GRANT TEXTBOOK SERIES

VOLUME III, SYNTHESIS OF THE HOROSCOPE

CATHARINE T. GRANT
AND
ERNEST A. GRANT

Copyright 1988 by the American Federation of Astrologers

No part of this book may be reproduced or transmitted in any form or by any means, electronic or mechanical, including photocopying or recording, or by any information storage and retrieval system, without written permission from the publisher. Requests and inquiries may be mailed to: American Federation of Astrologers, Inc., 6535 S. Rural Road, Tempe, AZ 85283.

First Printing: 1988
Current Printing: 2018

ISBN: 978-0-86690-343-1
LCC: 88-70466

Cover design: Jack Cipolla

Published by:
American Federation of Astrologers, Inc.
6535 S. Rural Road
Tempe, AZ 85283

www.astrologers.com

Contents

Chapter 1, Synthesizing the Character   1

Chapter 2, Determining the Character   25

Chapter 3: Life Expectancy   41

Chapter 4: Health Indicators   53

Chapter 5: Family Relationships   67

Chapter 6: Individual Relationships   87

Chapter 7: Love Relationships   105

Chapter 8: Marital Relationships   127

Chapter 9: Vocational Relationships   145

Chapter 10: Travel Relationships   161

| CHAPTER 1 |

SYNTHESIZING THE CHARACTER

AS POINTED OUT IN THE PREVIOUS volume, the first step in horoscopic interpretation is analysis of all the horoscope's component parts. These must necessarily be considered separately for they are a detailed determination of the influences indicated in the birth chart, as distinct from the latter's overall perspective. The material presented in the first two volumes is sufficient for this purpose. With some practice the student should be able to analyze a horoscope, but such analysis will necessarily be incomplete since each configuration will be considered separately from, and without relation to, the horoscope as a whole.

Horoscopic interpretation, however, is much more than this, for it must take into account influences upon man and life which are constantly changing, of divergent character, and at times seemingly opposed to each other. Reconciliation on an analytic basis then becomes difficult, for astrology deals with *all* the influences in an individual's life; 1) some of them will be minor, 2) some are minor but seem important to the native, 3) others are major, while still 4) others are major but may seem to be minor. Because every horoscope differs, at least slightly, from every other these difficulties mount until the student must ultimately consider each horoscope as a whole—synthesizing apparently contradictory influences into a total picture of the native's very existence. At this point the student truly becomes an artist.

Synthesis demands practice, far more than analysis which ultimately can be done using a good textbook. Practice, or clinical experience, develops the ability to balance and judge the respective weights of the various influences, thus seeing the chart as a whole and determining its meaning. While this may appear difficult to the beginner, it should not be allowed to become a discouragement, since it is a stage through which every student must pass. Instead of dampening enthusiasm, it should prove stimulus to more thorough study and investigation for nothing is as interesting as life itself.

Alan Leo, the great English astrologer of the late 19th and early 20th centuries, said: "There is really no one sure and certain method of overcoming these troubles. A good knowledge of the subject and practical experience are the only safe guides. The various rules given by ancient and modern authors are intended to point the way and to indicate what is likely to be the outcome of the many possible and divergent positions and aspects: in fact each rule is a short synthesis in itself."

No life is a series of unrelated events. Every event in a man's or woman's life is part of a whole and is related, to some degree, to every other event in that life. Each has a physical, psychological, and spiritual dimension, and, when a horoscope has been analyzed, it must not only be synthesized to set forth its harmony—it must be resynthesized in order to apply this harmonized analysis to the facts.

Life is complex, but the great majority of those who consult an astrologer have some particular, momentarily important, problem in mind. The person may not be interested in a complete character analysis. In the United States the average adult is less interested in personal character than in that of his children, as revealed by the horoscope. He may or may not want to know his ultimate destiny, but he is usually very interested in the specific problem of the moment.

A parent may inquire about a child's health when the child is ill and parents want to know when he will recover. Or the parent may want to know his offspring's vocational indicators. Another may inquire about personal health, finances, chance of promotion, or change in occupation. He is dissatisfied with the present job and wants to know whether to change now or wait. Another person may inquire about an emotional problem; he is contemplating marriage and wants to know if and when the step should be taken. Are the two horoscopes favorable for conjugal happiness? Many horoscopes of opposite sexes, while favoring lasting friendship, are not at all suitable for permanent and lasting marriage.

If the astrologer is to justify a client's confidence, he must be able to answer these and a thousand more questions. Experience with horoscopic delineation must make him a good psychologist, enabling him to appreciate the factors in the horoscope which affect the client's emotional relations. And the astrologer's conclusions must be based on a careful determination of all the astrological factors involved.

Every chart has its strengths and weaknesses. One chart may be strong as regards marriage and weak as regards wealth; another may be the reverse. The strong factors are usually much easier to determine, but even the more remote ones must be disclosed, as their proper understanding enables the competent astrologer to assist his client in developing weak characteristics whose enhancement will make his life more successful.

This requires not only a sound knowledge of astrology, but experience, good judgment, and a natural psychological bent. Success here comes through developing an astrological sense. While there are rules for synthesis, many of them useful, in the last resort synthesis is largely the astrologer's judgment based upon immutable laws—just as a physician's diagnosis is largely his or her own individual judgment rooted in his academic training and clinical experience. The competent astrologer does not merely record what has been found but out of these separate parts develops and creates the whole pattern of the native's life.

Even if the client is not interested in his own character, the astrologer must understand in order to correctly interpret the client's horoscope. Free will and individual choice must not be eliminated, for man is not an automation; his career and experiences are neither predetermined nor the result of chance. Not only will two persons react differently to similar circumstances, but the same person will react differently to the same circumstances at a different time. Therefore, in all delineations the native's character is of primary importance; all other determination of the native's future success or failure depends on it.

Many different techniques have been developed for determining the true character as revealed by the horoscope. Inherent qualities of character spring from heredity and environment, particularly the conditions surrounding the native in his early or formative years of life. However, this is not invariably true, since in some instances the native's whole character has changed after maturity—often through a profound spiritual experience. But the horoscope itself, when carefully analyzed and synthesized, will show all of these factors.

No claims for complete originality are made in behalf of the technique presented in the following pages. Probably 90 percent of any astrologer's knowledge is derived from great minds which have preceded him. But interwoven in this technique is the author's own experience, and after all, the only things we truly know are those personally experienced.

The starting point for any determination of character must necessarily be the Ascendant, plus the Sun and Moon positions; also, the position of the ruler of the Ascendant must be taken into consideration. While Jupiter in Sagittarius possesses some definite power which is by and large the same in all horoscopes (analysis), it will have a different effect on the person born with Sagittarius rising than on the person born with Cancer, Leo, or any other sign rising. Similarly, Venus in the Ascendant is always fortunate, but its influence is manifested differently when it is rising in Taurus or Libra than when rising in Aries or Scorpio.

However, while these factors are important, the author has discovered by experience that the qualities of action (quadruplicities) and the planes of action (triplicities) through which the native expresses himself are the first aspects of the character to be considered. If there is no balance here, there can be no balance in the inherent qualities of character shown in the natal chart. Through understanding of the causes that are out of balance, the astrologer can help the client develop the characteristics which, in some measure at least, help bring about a balance. The qualities of action are shown through the quadruplicity positions of the celestial bodies as a whole at the moment of birth, while the planes of action are shown through the triplicities.

In reference to the quadruplicities and triplicities, Alan Leo once wrote, "This (the quadruplicities and triplicities) seems to be the best method suggested up to the moment of giving a general view of the type of horoscope as a whole; the number of planets in signs of fire, earth, air, and water will show which triplicity is strongest; the number of movable, fixed, and common signs will indicate the predominant quadruplicity; and finally the juxtaposition of these two results will make still more definite the type of the whole."

Quadruplicities or Qualities of Action

As was discussed in Volume I and shown in Table 1, the quadruplicities are a threefold division of the signs of the zodiac: cardinal, fixed, and mutable. Careful attention to the planetary groupings in these divisions of the heavens will well repay the astrologer, for they are an important clue to unraveling the mysteries of the horoscope. Whether used for good or evil will depend on the native's character as determined through synthesis with the triplicities.

Table I. Zodiacal Sign Affinities					
Zodiac Sign	Quadruplicity Quality of Action	Triplicity Plane of Action	Trinity Mode of Action	Receptivity	Direction or Ecliptic
Aries	Cardinal	Fire	Intellectual	+	Northern
Taurus	Fixed	Earth	Intellectual	−	Northern
Gemini	Mutable	Air	Intellectual	+	Northern
Cancer	Cardinal	Water	Maternal	−	Northern
Leo	Fixed	Fire	Maternal	+	Northern
Virgo	Mutable	Earth	Maternal	−	Northern
Libra	Cardinal	Air	Reproductive	+	Southern
Scorpio	Fixed	Water	Reproductive	−	Southern
Sagittarius	Mutable	Fire	Reproductive	+	Southern
Capricorn	Cardinal	Earth	Serving	−	Southern
Aquarius	Fixed	Air	Serving	+	Southern
Pisces	Mutable	Water	Serving	−	Southern

If most of the planets are located in one of the three triplicities, the native will be strongly impressed with that particular quality; it will constitute the personality or temperament. Three characteristic temperaments correspond to these three qualities:

Cardinal: Ascendant, Action
Fixed: Sun, Will
Mutable: Moon, Wisdom

Cardinal Temperament

The cardinal temperament increases the native's activities in whatever sphere is indicated by other factors in the chart. These individuals have strong wills, ambitious personalities, and dynamic energy. Quoting again from Alan Leo, "The active temperament is bestowed when the majority of planets are in cardinal signs. This is perhaps the most pronounced and acute of the three groups, and stands for energy, activity, change, ardor, enthusiasm—self-consciousness realized in a life of action. Persons with this temperament are easily spurred to activity, either by force of circumstance or by their own inherent nature; and they generally come more or less prominently before the world because they prefer a life of action to inaction."

This gives the practical man or the man of action. The cardinal signs also give opportunity, for the person of action creates opportunity. Leo says again, "They produce a reforming and pioneering spirit, with readiness of response to changes in the world around them."

If the horoscope shows the character to be undeveloped or of a low order, the evil side of this temperament emerges and the native is unstable, restless, excitable, full of unwise enthusiasm, and lacking in caution. Aims and interests in life are frustrated by ill-regulated activity; change occurs without reason.

Of course, the astrologer must pinpoint the nature of the separate signs, for a grouping of planets in cardinal Capricorn will necessarily operate differently from a grouping in Libra, Cancer, or Aries.

In Aries planets indicate impulsiveness and excitability, with a desire to be at the forefront. The native is very self-assertive. A predominance of bodies in cardinal Aries given intense devotion to persons or causes but also a liability to enmity through aggressive or argumentative forcefulness.

Many planets in Cancer cause silent ambition and quiet

persistence. The energies are conserved and feeling plays a prominent part. The emotional side of the nature plays a leading part in the ambition, and the native frequently acts on hunches.

Libra planets bring a type of cooperative ambition not found elsewhere in the horoscope. While the native's activity is largely intellectual, imagination and artistry are also important. Here is devotion to ideals rather than to causes, although the ideal may be embodied in a person or a cause.

Planets in Capricorn indicate a person of steady resolution who is active in science and politics. These are more practical than Cancer or Libra and are better to implement their ambitions in everyday practice. Many planets in cardinal Capricorn give self-will and egoism, but the native wants to work for the multitude rather than for the few. Hence it is a political sign.

In the United States, Saturn thus symbolizes the Democratic Party; while the wealth and expansive nature of Sagittarius cause Jupiter to be the symbol of the Republican Party. Personal ambitions are also strong, particularly if personal planets are found herein.

When extremists have their planets largely grouped in the cardinal signs, their careers are more or less public.

Fixed Temperament

Fixed temperament occurs when a majority of the planets are in fixed signs. These persons are the opposite of the cardinal type in that their principal characteristics are firmness, inertia, stability, fixity, and dislike of change. They are orthodox and easily get into a rut. This is often coupled with great determination plus a dogmatic outlook.

The native is thorough and painstaking in everything, always completing every task. Whether or not this unyielding temperament works for good or evil depends largely on the native's moral development.

Natives with many planets in fixed signs are generally organizers and builders. Being steady and persistent, they are also accumulators. They do not scatter their efforts, but rather concentrate them. In the higher plane these qualities benefit the native by leading to cultivation of good traits; in the lower plane, however, they produce indolence, obstinacy, stubbornness, and bigotry.

If the fixed chart indicates a strong intellectual nature, the native has a profound and all-encompassing mind with good memory and the ability to deal with broad or comprehensive subjects.

While these fixed signs develop strength of will, self-control, and mastery over self and others, they also indicate pride (particularly Taurus) and dignity. Their slowness and practicality cause the native to follow mechanical, artistic, and trading vocations, usually in responsible positions since he is conservative, thorough, and well-meaning.

If many planets are grouped in Taurus, this fixity is even more apparent and is sometimes accompanied by an inclination to jealousy (in petty affairs), stubbornness, obstinacy, or pride.

Where many planets are grouped in Leo, the native loves power and authority. He is determined and persistent but emotionally ardent. Being the natural sign of the Sun, Leo gives more self-reliance and self-assurance than any other placement. These people are often very austere or, at the other extreme, very gracious.

The positive side of the nature stands out with many planets grouped in Scorpio. Pride is found here, coupled with extravagance. The elements of resentment and vindictiveness in the Scorpio character often hinder proper development. In contrast to Leo, which gives love of leadership, Scorpio gives the lower side of this characteristic—love of domination.

The native who has many planets grouped in Aquarius has

a very unusual temperament, difficult to understand because of its originality which is often far in advance of his generation. This temperament has a refining element, but the fixedness of the native's mind (it is an air sign) often causes him to run in a groove. These persons are very agreeable and companionable when once known, but quite decided in their opinions. They will carry on with their own plans, quietly and without fanfare, undeterred by opposition or even unpopularity.

Mutable Temperament

The mutable temperament is the harmonious temperament. When many planets are grouped in a mutable sign, it indicates harmony and peace rather than discord and strife - to such a point that the native may have a rather monotonous disposition.

The mutable temperament has a greater affinity with the intellectual life than either of the other quadruplicities. Alan Leo writes that this temperament is often unfit for work in the world unless accompanied by a cardinal quality. But the fact is that they can adjust or adapt themselves to almost any contingency, and this flexibility is frequently their best quality.

The intellect conferred by a mutable temperament can be superficial, changeable, and impractical; or profound, stable, and all-encompassing; much depending upon the triplicities in which the planets are found. The native's finesse and subtlety are often wholesome qualities, but in charts of lower development these may become craftiness, cunning, and deceit. Lack of candor and duplicity in the lower plane become, on the higher, insight, understanding, and ability to see beneath the surface. The native is often highly intuitive and may even seem to be ruled by it, but this should not be confused with emotionalism.

The mutable quality tends to develop a methodical, sympathetic, sensitive, nervous, and highly-strung nature. Unless the chart is otherwise strong, there is a tendency to irresolution, vacillation, and lack of responsibility. Support from the other signs is required for the mutable signs to display their best side. Adaptability, intellectual ability, and ingenuity are fine qualities when used to good purpose, but in a lower nature these can cause much harm.

When many planets are found in either Gemini or Virgo, the two mercurial signs of this quadruplicity, there is a strong tendency to worry, anxiety, daydreaming, and absentmindedness, unless counteracted by other strong influences. Because of the peculiar variability of Mercury's nature, much depends on this planet's position in the chart. It is somewhat reflected in these two signs: both inclining to intellectual ability, with Gemini more literary and philosophical and Virgo more scientific.

The author disagrees with those astrological authors who claim that both Gemini and Virgo indicate a critical nature, without a more explicit definition of critical. Persons with many planets in Gemini are usually quick to see all sides of an issue and thus express themselves quickly and forcefully (although not always correctly). This is sometimes misconstrued as criticism. Virgo, on the other hand, is deeply analytical, and the native may be destructively critical in the worst sense of the word. This is far different from a criticism which builds.

Gemini and Virgo tend naturally to attach themselves to other stronger wills—not as parasites but in a way designed to assist and develop. Thus these natives quickly form friendships and partnerships. They are companionable and devoted, with a sociability based upon understanding more than emotion. Hence they are difficult to understand and one can live with them for years without fully knowing them.

When many planets are found in mutable Sagittarius or in Pisces, the native is superficially more open than with any other sign. With a chart well-balanced, natives are also well-balanced, harmonious, and peaceable. A Sagittarius is formal and precise, while a Pisces inclines to fine etiquette, fine clothes, pomp, and show. Sagittarius is orthodox and philosophical, while Pisces is mystical and philosophical.

Much care must be exercised in connection with Sagittarius, for planets posited therein, and out of harmony with it, will upset the whole nature. For instance, Sagittarius in itself produces the formal, orthodox, and philosophical type. But Mars in Sagittarius will often make the native rash, perverse, and rebellious against orthodoxy. The Martian influence in Pisces makes the native indolent, placid, and indifferent. Pisces leans to the psychic, while Sagittarius inclines to orthodox religious experience.

Thus, the positions of the planets in the three quadruplicities are a strong clue to the horoscope as a whole, and this can be seen even before the horoscope is considered further. To sum up, the cardinal qualities are quickening, energizing, and active; the fixed qualities are stable and firm, apt to remain latent and inert; while the mutable qualities are harmonious and flexible.

Triplicities or Planes of Action

To the ancient astrologers all matter or physical manifestation was divided into the four basic elements: earth, fire, air, and water (see Table I). Even though science today classifies matter into six categories, for astrological purposes it is more practical to follow the principles laid down by the ancients and regard matter as a mixture of the four elements. Modern science may ultimately classify matter into twelve basic categories and thus unwittingly provide a broader base for the classification of individual signs than the sign rulership of the elements used at present.

As single keyword types the quadruplicities may be classified as active, fixed, and harmonizing. But whether these characteristics will be for good or ill will depend largely upon their relationship to the planes of action as shown by the triplicities

No horoscope is perfect, just as no life is perfect, for the former portrays the latter. But, leaving aside house position, the more equal the distribution of planets over the chart, the greater is the likelihood that the life will be harmonious unless distribution causes the planets to fall in one or more of the triplicities or quadruplicities to the detriment of the other triplicities or quadruplicities. This will be better understood when the following pages have been read and checked against familiar horoscopes.

Fiery Triplicity

The fiery triplicity is essentially mental or psychological in nature. The signs composing it— Aries, Leo, and Sagittarius—are masculine (or positive); each representing energy, self-reliance, self-assertiveness, and action. The triplicity as a whole represents the spirit of leadership, control, and advance. Every philosophy known to history has posited fire as the principle of life: thus, this triplicity as a unit is creative, sustaining, and transmuting. The native's character is directed to mental activities. He thinks, uses his head instead of brawn, and is guided by reason. The individual is aggressive and forward, so his character and personality have nothing static about them.

Of course, these are the characteristics of the pure type with equalized distribution of the planets. Such a pure type is rare but the blending with the qualities of action is discussed later.

Earthy Triplicity

The earthy triplicity is materialistic in outlook. Represented by Taurus, Virgo, and Capricorn, not only is this type of character practical, proud, and stable; but the native is a physical rather than a mental worker. While there are exceptions to this rule, of course, for it is the exception which really brings forth the rule. The native must be able to feel things physically; mental or psychological reaction is not enough. He or she does not appreciate a home unless experiencing it physically. This all lends a certain self-righteousness to the native's character, but he is dependable, because of the staying qualities so often missing in the other triplicities. Usually slow to learn, the native maintains a course until it succeeds without deviating to one side or the other; liking to follow a given path and obey the rules. They are difficult to deal with as children, for care must be taken not to break the native's will. These people are much more easily led than driven, so appeal to pride will often be effective. Objectives in life are obtained through tenacity, but the student should again be warned that lack of balance in the chart may cause the native to select inferior objectives.

Airy Triplicity

The airy triplicity produces harmony or disharmony. Composed of Gemini, Libra, and Aquarius, this element is more akin to the mental (fiery) triplicity and mental characteristics than either earth or water and, although each of these signs expresses a dual quality, it is nonetheless a triplicity of unification in its primary expression. Just as the air permeates and penetrates all space, the artistic and refined airy triplicity has its plane of action in fraternizing, harmonizing, and blending. The airy temperament is the diplomat who intervenes between conflicting elements and unites them. When too well-balanced, however, this temperament suffers from inertia and the over-confidence that begets failure. He expects all things to come to him.

Watery Triplicity

The watery triplicity acts as psychic, emotional, impermanent, and unchanging. Thus, the expression of Cancer, Scorpio, and Pisces has always been one of emotion and feeling. When well-balanced it is one of adjustment and, whether balanced or not, it acts through emotional response far more than through the intellect, materialistic desires, or urge for unification. Furthermore, emotional reactions manifest greater extremes than any other grouping and the native is either a profound, sincere, and well-balanced spiritual person, or he is hesitating, equivocating, emotional, and unreliable. Sensation (not necessarily sensationalism) is the very key to existence, and the native is often quite intuitive, acting through hunches, emotions, and intuitive perceptions more than by reasoning or logical deduction. Balance is the quality most needed in this triplicity, more than in any other, for its absence only too often causes indecision in the most important matters of life; the native becomes psychopathic and requires psychiatric attention to restore his normal plane of expression or action.

Qualities and Planes of Action Combined

In order to keep this study succinct and readily understandable, the following material only presents combinations of the quadruplicities with the triplicities though such pure types, lacking other qualities and planes of action needed for fine balance, are actually rare. By balance the author, of course, means an equal distribution of the Sun, Moon, and planets over the quadruplicities and triplicities with each celestial body in the particular sign, quadruplicity, and triplicity with which it is naturally most in harmony. The planets can be easily seen when placed in a graphic form such as Table 2.

Table 2. Essence of the Native				
	Fire	Earth	Air	Water
Cardinal				
Fixed				
Mutable				

Cardinal Fire

The cardinal-fire combination shows an energetic character and independence in both thought and action; these persons function mainly on the mental plane, have very quick perception, readily grasp a factual situation, and have wonderful mental abilities where mastery of detail is not required. They usually see the end from the beginning, rather than the steps in between. This combination is usually harmonious, with talent, high ideals, plus the ability to respond. The native is conscious of his abilities, so the slightest lack of balance in the chart can give rise to egoism which proves a hindrance to advancement. They are intellectually active, sincere, and progressive, making wonderful teachers, despite a tendency to pugnacity. These individuals are sincere in advocating their personal views.

Cardinal Earth

The cardinal-earth combination produces the ambitious character who is practical and sincere but usually more interested in the materialistic or physical. Being prudent, reserved, and cautious, this type is often regarded as slow, but the key is active stability: the native, although progressive, is persevering and holds fast to that which is established before venturing into new fields.

Since their number one priority is protecting personal material, financial, or other interests, they seem (and sometimes are) selfish. Unlike the other cardinal combinations, these natives can take the good as well as the bad; when there is lack of balance, the bad produces a type of pessimism which impedes the development of good character. The native is crafty, accepts the principle that self-preservation is the first law of nature, and unhesitatingly looks out for himself at all times.

Cardinal Air

The cardinal-air combination receives little understanding because of the speed with which it acts. The native's intentions are always good but they are misunderstood, and he suffers from a desire to harmonize and reconcile all those with whom he is in contact.

Being a peacemaker, honest and reliable, with a highly developed intuition, the native is absorbed in the desire to unify and perfect. These persons are invariably refined, usually better than their environment, and never inferior to it. The ambition which marks all cardinal combinations is here channeled toward causes to represent, ideals to support, and individuals with whom to associate, rather than toward personal life and fate. Knowing instinctively that they help self through helping others, they are usually dispassionate, cool, and collected, but withal firm, active, and forward looking. However, this character is also inclined to nervousness. They make good politicians, statesmen, representatives of organizations, and public relations specialists.

Cardinal Water

The cardinal-water combination produces sensitive individual with exalted social ambitions, deep feelings, and much sympathy. Lacking the stability of fire, earth, or air, the character is somewhat changeable. Emotion is more important than intellect. Being affectionate, he can demand and secure the affection of others. Sometimes he displays affections too strongly, wearing his heart on his sleeve so to speak, and thus inclined to sentimentality. Emotionalism means that successful romance is very important to him and may, indeed, determine his whole course of life. Conversely, the disruption of a romance or a blocking of the native's emotions can lead him into a world of unreality. In a well-balanced chart, however, the character is deeply sympathetic, and pride in successful accomplishment knows no bounds.

Fixed Fire

The fixed-fire combination produces a character which never succumbs to failure; if not a big fish in a big pond, the native will at least be a big fish in a little pond. His tenacity, determination, and elevated character are indeed wonderful assets. This person is strong-willed and quietly ambitious, rarely pushing himself forward. Yet he usually ends in a position of leadership through inherent ability to use the talents of others, managing and guiding them by enormous administrative ability. He is conscientious, loyal, determined, and trustworthy; he is personally magnetic to the point, when this quality is highly developed, of being able to magnetize others in turn. But withal the mental outlook is philosophical and practical. A well-balanced fixed-fire individual rarely fails in anything.

Fixed Earth

The fixed-earth combination is one of the most difficult to deal with because of its materialism, obstinacy, rigid inflexibility, and pride. Much depends upon the planetary configurations, and great caution must be exercised in judging the native's innate character. Being proud with much self-esteem, he is also slow, plodding, and cautious. This individual is often suspicious of the motives of others. Alan Leo says of this type, "It may be termed a critical combination in which the limitations of fate are more marked than in other combinations." But, the author's experience holds that the fate to which Leo refers means the doggedness of these individuals and their tenacity in holding firm to what they have or believe. They are materialistic in the extreme but, strangely enough, when this combination balances with cardinal fire in their charts, it usually brings high psychic abilities as well (through steady application of the principles of development).

Fixed Air

The fixed-air combination produces a dignified and noble character who is often misunderstood; while making a poor first impression, he improves upon acquaintance. He is refined, trustworthy, and aristocratic, always earnest and serious, and lacking in any facetiousness. Being conservative and selective he chooses his associates carefully; he is restrictive and follows custom except when it suits his purposes to advance himself (the chart is then invariably out of balance). Coupled with all of this is a stabilizing quality which produces harmony, although the establishment of this harmony may take considerable time.

Fixed Water

The fixed-water combination produces a strongly emotional type whose feelings run to extremes, either loving or hating fiercely. The character is hard to understand, even when analyzed by a good psychologist, but astrology holds the key to it. The native loves to appear mystical or mysterious; but is jealous, suspicious, and mistrustful. Imagination often runs riot, thus making life miserable for himself and his associates. The fixed quality of action in the plane of water must be balanced by other strong factors if the character is to be of the higher type; consequently these persons are frequently the victims of temptations which, one after the other, have a fateful impact on their lives. They are ardent but possessive in their affections.

Mutable Fire

The mutable-fire combination produces a demonstrative character with violent expression of likes, dislikes, emotions, and feeling. While the native's characteristics are fundamentally mental, he is nervous and tends to diffuse energies and scatter interests. When balanced, these persons are usually talented, honest, generous, and warm-hearted; otherwise they are eccentric irritable and wasteful. A blend of fixed-air with this type is very helpful as it stabilizes this character and focuses the native's interests, ensuring that his great energy produces results.

Mutable Earth

The mutable-earth combination is another temperament that clashes with itself. The native appears to be quick but is actually slow and reserved in opinions and expressions, too frequently lacking candor. A dearth of willpower easily makes the native a victim of habit. Indifference is the keynote here, although the native's analytical ability often leads to action with favorable results. They are methodical, to the point of monotony. Opportunities are usually lacking, since chance is generated by the native, and these persons do not have the necessary qualities.

Mutable Air

The mutable-air combination finds intellectual ability woven into character. The native is interested in scientific and intellectual pursuits but must continually struggle within to overcome a natural indifference not conducive to either character development and success in life. In this combination, more than in any other, environment plays a major role in character development. The native seems to absorb his surroundings or, rather, the environment penetrates his character and becomes a part of it. They can be refined and elegant or sharp, rude, and disdainful; there is seldom a middle ground.

Mutable Water

The mutable-water combination is the most fortunate of all. Being feminine, negative, and passive, it is better adapted to women than to men, in the latter giving rise to a parasite or leaning type. These persons are very sensitive to the environment and easily taken in by others. They are fretful and capricious, so the planetary positions must be studied carefully to reach a correct judgment of the horoscope. Any stabilizing combination is beneficial when interwoven here with this character and tends to elevate and strengthen the native's character through our life. For the character is inherently weak unless strengthened by the upbringing in the early years of life. The native absorbs his environment.

Few horoscopes will manifest only one of the foregoing combinations. Character is determined by balancing and synthesizing various combination and their tendencies. Table 2 can be used as an easy way to combine the factors. But the first step is to delineate the true characteristics shown in the quadruplicities and the triplicities, as this is the proper foundation for a correct delineation or synthesis of the horoscope as shown in Figure 1 and Table 3. Never make the common mistake of judging a person's character by his acts. Character goes deeper than that.

Acts are the manifestations of character, but character itself is the deeper emotion which prompts the individual to act as he does. Result: Cardinal-Fire.

Table 3. Character Determination for Figure 1 Example.				
	Fire	Earth	Water	Air
Cardinal	☽ ☉ ☿	♂		♀
Fixed	♆	♀		♄
Mutable	♃	Asc	MC	♅

These combinations are to some extent expressed outwardly by the house positions of the planets ruling them (Table 4), for the modes of action are found through the houses. Thus Mars in the first house in any sign (this house being angular) takes on some of the characteristics usually assigned to cardinal signs; but it also retains some of the coloring of Aries when in

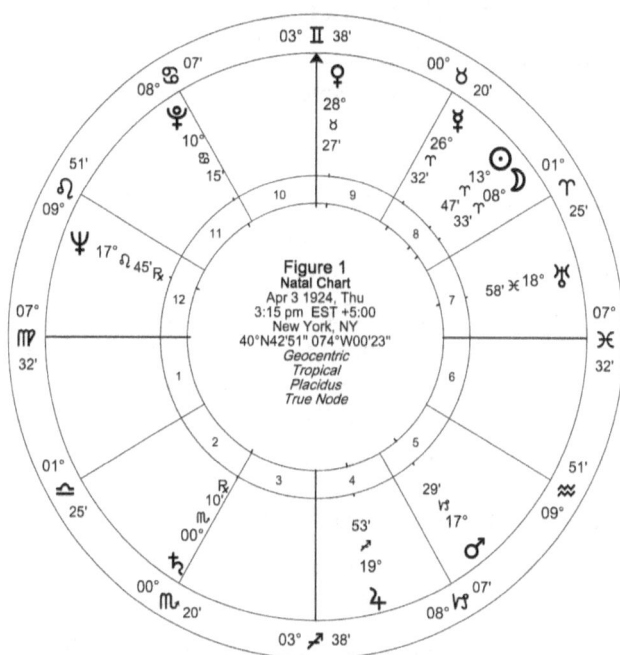

Figure 1
Natal Chart
Apr 3 1924, Thu
3:15 pm EST +5:00
New York, NY
40°N42'51" 074°W00'23"
Geocentric
Tropical
Placidus
True Node

the first house, so its makeup includes the cardinal-fire combination harmonious to Mars.

Table 4. Rulership Pattern.					
Planets	Symbol	Rule	Detriment	Exaltation	Fall
Sun	☉	♌	♒	♈	♎
Moon	☽	♋	♑	♉	♏
Mercury	☿	♊ ♍	♐ ♓	♒	♌
Venus	♀	♉ ♎	♏ ♈	♓	♍
Mars	♂	♈	♎	♑	♋
Jupiter	♃	♐	♊	♋	♑
Saturn	♄	♑	♋	♎	♈
Uranus	♅	♒	♌	♏	♉
Neptune	♆	♓	♍	♐	♊
Pluto	♀	♏	♉	♌	♒

Remember that this chapter did not deal with aspects of the planets, which is another matter entirely and of lesser importance. In a balanced character, benefic aspects are heightened in their power for good; while the same inherently good aspects in an unbalanced character may prove the undoing of the native and the neutralization of any inherent good qualities.

Henceforth, a study of synthesis will take up the various phases of life itself rather than the qualities (character) that enter into the completion of that life. No longer considering the planes of action of character, now it is time to take up the avenues of action or expression of the life behind the character.

Review Questions for Chapter 1

1. Define the difference between analyzing the horoscope and synthesizing it.

2. Is it important to completely delineate the client's horoscope

even though he or she has a single question of interest at the moment? Why?

3. Write the combinations of the quadruplicities and the triplicities in your own words or keywords.

4. Calculate the following horoscope and then determine the character or essence. Does it differ from the Sun sign or Ascendant sign? Merv Griffen, entertainer and TV host, July 6, 1925, San Mateo, California, 4:45 a.m. PST.

| Chapter 2 |

Determining the Character

This course of study may seem to overemphasize the native's character. This is because the author has found that too little attention is paid initially to the native's character, leading to poor horoscope delineation. Hence, attention must be directed again and again to the complex factors in every horoscope that determine character and thus express the native's attitude toward life itself.

An analysis of the influence upon character of the Sun, Moon, Mercury, and Ascendant is insufficient, since they only determine the foundation upon which character is built. However, these bodies are fundamental since their zodiacal positions and aspects indicate the native's hereditary character traits while house positions and aspects largely determine environmental influences on character.

But synthesis requires a deeper search of the horoscope. The qualities of action indicate the creative, stable, and harmonic dimensions of the native's character. The planes of action show the individual's affinity for mental, physical, emotional, and intuitional expressions. Together, these factors have been shown to determine the basic temperament.

However, there are yet other factors of the horoscope to be considered. The trinities, or modes of action, indicate the path through which the temperament is expressed. These are basically intellectual, maternal, reproductive, and leaning, or serving.

The balance of the native is also determined by weighing the power of the four quadrants of the natal horoscope. Having groups of planets predominantly in either a single quadrant or a single hemisphere gives far-reaching implications.

The Sun's zodiacal position (decanate, facet, and sign; see Table 5) indicates the ego or inner self, while the Moon reflects the inner self as expressed in personality. Similarly, Mercury is the key to the native's mentality although it does not indicate mental ability alone. As already mentioned, Mercury's nature is neutral, and it takes on the quality of that luminary or planet whose aspect influences it most strongly for good or evil. It often takes on the combined qualities of two or more celestial bodies.

Uranus, Neptune, and Pluto, insofar as character is concerned, are higher octaves of Mercury, Venus, and Mars, and Uranus and Neptune are esoterically octaves of the Sun and Moon. When zodiacal and house positions and aspects are considered, Uranus, Neptune, and Pluto are found to supply the key to the relationship between the subconscious and the conscious self.

The polarities give clues to the native's powers of reception, and the dominant water signs also indicate receptivity. The word, *polarity* must be defined as it is used in astrology. In astrology, as in physics, the polarity simply denotes the tendency of a group of two or more planets to arrange themselves in some relationship or geometric pattern with respect to one another. The term is often used incorrectly and, for example, a pair of opposites alone may (erroneously) be considered a polarity.

When these factors have been weighed, the Ascendant enables the astrologer to sum up the remainder of the horoscope, since this is the detailed foundation upon which most of the detailed interpretation must rest. Since the ascending sign, in its decanate and facet, relates to the native's self-consciousness, this is the clue to the signs on every other house cusp.

Table 5. Sign Decanate Rulerships			
Zodiac Sign	Decanates		
	First, 1-10°	Second, 11-20°	Third, 21-30°
Aries	Mars - Mars	Mars - Sun	Mars - Jupiter
Taurus	Venus - Venus	Venus - Mercury	Venus - Saturn
Gemini	Mercury - Mercury	Mercury - Venus	Mercury - Uranus
Cancer	Moon - Moon	Moon - Pluto	Moon - Neptune
Leo	Sun - Sun	Sun - Jupiter	Sun - Mars
Virgo	Mercury - Mercury	Mercury - Saturn	Mercury - Venus
Libra	Venus - Venus	Venus - Uranus	Venus - Mercury
Scorpio	Pluto - Pluto	Pluto - Neptune	Pluto - Moon
Sagittarius	Jupiter - Jupiter	Jupiter - Mars	Jupiter - Sun
Capricorn	Saturn - Saturn	Saturn - Venus	Saturn - Mercury
Aquarius	Uranus - Uranus	Uranus - Mercury	Uranus - Venus
Pisces	Neptune - Neptune	Neptune - Moon	Neptune - Pluto

In synthesizing character the astrologer must have even broader horizons, since he must be able to interpret properly the tripartite division of intellect, emotions, and actions which are the psychologically governing conditions of character. Information obtained by applying the above paragraphs to the horoscope must be considered in relationship to each of these divisions.

Hemispheres

The houses of the horoscope are divided into four major quadrants which compare with the trinities of the zodiac signs. In addition, the houses are split into hemispheres, from north to south and also from east to west as shown in Figure 2, below, four quadrants of the horoscope showing quadrant and hemisphere emphasis.

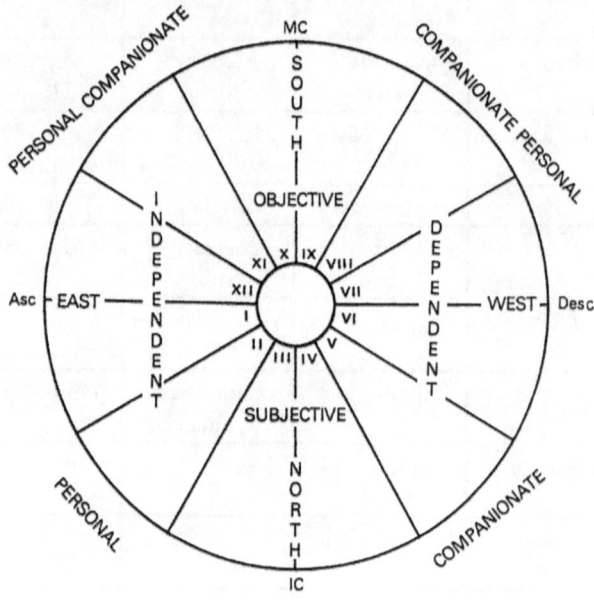

The eastern hemisphere extends from houses X through II, counterclockwise, which corresponds to signs Capricorn through Gemini. Planets placed in this half of the horoscope show where the native is capable of directing his own activities and functioning independently. When a predominance of planets are found in the east, or oriental, side of the nativity the person is said to be in control of his own destiny. This native initiates procedures rather than waiting for events to occur. In psychological terms the person is called an extrovert.

When planets are located in the western hemisphere, ranging from house four through house nine, counterclockwise, the native responds to the demands of his environment. This individual is primarily a product of the times rather than master of his own ship. An introverted personality such as this often seems dependent upon his associates for direction. This occidental hemisphere equals signs Cancer through Sagittarius of the natural zodiac.

To determine the hemisphere emphasis merely add the number of planets located in each area and note them as E/W.

Looking at the horoscope circle in another way it can be divided between north and south. The northern hemisphere runs from house one through house six, counterclockwise, which relates to signs Aries through Virgo. Planets placed in the north show where the native is related to personal concerns and where he looks at life in a subjective way. Often this area deals with invisible or spiritual matters.

The houses which are in the southern hemisphere are seven through twelve, corresponding to Libra through Pisces. This southern hemisphere of the horoscope deals with public matters and reacts in an objective or impersonal manner. Planets posited here show concern with practical and visible activities.

The balance between north and south is found by totaling the number of planets in each hemisphere and noting them as N/S. A predominance of planets placed in the south indicates that life will be open to public scrutiny and personal efforts will be made on behalf of others. Whereas, a horoscope having more planets in the north will lead an obscure existence and efforts will be for self.

Quadrants and Trinities

Since the division of the quadrants and trinities is so closely aligned they may be considered together with the reminder that the signs do not always reside in their natural houses.

The first three houses of the horoscope, related to the zodiac signs of Aries, Taurus, and Gemini, are grouped as Intellectual or Personal modes of action. This is at once both an active and a personal placement showing the natural self-expression of the client. Planets placed here give active and unsophisticated behavior. This space is often compared with the spring of the year when potential is being nurtured and developed, or with the planning session of a board where ideas are bursting forth. Instinctive reactions come out easily here.

Next follow houses four, five, and six, which relate to signs Cancer, Leo, and Virgo. This companionate area of the horoscope is more receptive and emotional without the energy and vitality of the earlier quadrant. This emotionally passive quarter of the chart will be aroused at a slower rate than other areas, so potential promised by resident planets may be realized later in life. Early relationships and training are shown in here so it is the first of the relating spheres. The native passively accepts or extends maternal care from or for another.

In houses seven through nine, or signs Libra, Scorpio, and Sagittarius, the native begins to arouse from his passive state and relate to the world around him on an equal basis. Planets posited here show emotional and physical receptivity but a mental outgoingness. The companion leads and the native follows. This trinity is called Reproductive and relates to the autumn of the year when the fruits of personal labor are harvested.

Last is found the trinity of houses 10 through 12, or signs Capricorn, Aquarius, and Pisces, where all personal concerns are set aside for the greater good of humanity. This independent, subjective area finds the native active on all three levels of emotional, physical, and mental expression. His interests are unselfish and he is capable of either leading or serving. Planets found here are usually expressing their higher vibration or potential. The personal-companionate quadrant is often called Serving.

A predominance of planets posited in any quadrant shows

emphasis through that path of expression. If the planets and signs found in a particular quadrant are in harmony with its direction all is in balance; however, if there is a divergence of these energies conflict will result. For example, energetic Mars would blend better in the first or the last quadrant than in either of the other two, whereas Saturn could easily be at home in all but the first quadrant of expression.

Receptivity

Each planet and sign has a positive and a masculine vibration or else a feminine and a negative vibration. This does not mean that they are good or bad but simply reflects the duality of this universe. Masculine, or positive, is aggressive and outgoing, while feminine is recessive and receptive. The planets are shown in Table 6. A balanced person will have an equal number of both positive and negative traits.

Table 6. Complementary Pairs of Planets.	
Positive Planets	*Negative Planets*
Sun	Moon
Mercury	Asteroid Belt
Mars	Venus
Jupiter	Saturn
Uranus	Neptune
Pluto	Transpluto

The positive vibration wants to influence those around him without yielding any of his personal will. He wants to form and keep his own opinions and feelings unchallenged by associates. This drive is what accomplishes tasks and creates goals. When a feminine planet such as the Moon or Venus is natally posited in a masculine sign there is naturally a confusion of the expression of this normally passive planet.

The negative, or feminine, method of expressing is to be agreeable and adaptable. These positions show open minds, desire for compromise to bring harmony, intuition, sympathy for other people, as well as laziness and sloth. The feminine planet or sign expresses best when associated with others. This explains why masculine Mars cannot feel at home in extremely feminine sign Taurus.

When a horoscope has a large grouping of either positive or negative planets by sign position it signifies a basic imbalance of the character. Also, the criteria which society has established for men and women are sometimes at odds with the temperament found in the natal horoscope. For example, a man having seven planets in feminine signs will react less aggressively than he is expected to behave according to social rules. Conversely, a woman having a majority of her planets in masculine signs will not be shy and compliant, especially if there are feminine planets. These factors are important when considering marital relationships.

Intellect

As already noted, Mercury plays an important part in the determination of intellectual qualities. As a neutral planet, its strength is derived first from its zodiacal position and secondly from its house position. Aspects from other celestial bodies must be considered in connection with the nature of the planet forming the aspect. If harmonious to the sign in which Mercury is located (and to a lesser extent, Mercury's house), the fact of its being a malefic aspect will not necessarily indicate a weak intellect; by the same token, a harmonious aspect will not in itself necessarily indicate that the native has a strong intellect.

The art of synthesis plays an important part. Mercury is naturally strong in Gemini and Virgo, also in Aquarius (the sign of its higher octave). In any sign it may give good intelligence if strongly and favorably aspected, but the sign itself is important since zodiacal position indicates the native's mode of intellectual expression. When well aspected and strongly influenced, Mercury expresses itself through intellect in each of the signs as follows:

Mercury in Aries gives an aggressive and dynamic intellect.

Mercury in Taurus gives a persistent and proud intellect.

Mercury in Gemini gives a brilliant, but too frequently superficial, intellect.

Mercury in Cancer gives a creative and imaginative intellect.

Mercury in Leo gives an authoritarian and determined intellect.

Mercury in Virgo gives a scientific and critical intellect.

Mercury in Libra gives a judicious and discriminating intellect.

Mercury in Scorpio gives an inquisitive and secretive intellect.

Mercury in Sagittarius gives an expansive and prophetic intellect.

Mercury in Capricorn gives an ambitious and practical intellect.

Mercury in Aquarius gives an original and occult intellect.

Mercury in Pisces gives a mystical and penetrating intellect.

When weak and inharmoniously aspected, Mercury will reveal the lower sides of these qualities. For example, when strongly and beneficially aspected in Leo, it is authoritarian and determined, but when weakly or malefically aspected, the intellect is expressed as domineering and stubborn.

Nor should it be forgotten that Mercury's position in a house indicates an intellect similar, although in a lesser degree, to the sign of that house. Thus, in the first house there is some correspondence to Aries; in the second, to Taurus, etc. Furthermore, Mercury is naturally stronger in houses three, six, and eleven, corresponding to Gemini, Virgo, and Aquarius. If strong in the third house, the intellect may be directed to the family, genealogy, and mental pursuits. In house six it may be directed to research, mathematics, and service of the kind indicated by sign and aspect. In house eleven it may be directed to the fraternal goodwill of Aquarius (badly aspected for extreme individualism), friendship, and occult interests. While Mercury in the first house would also direct the native's intellect toward relationships with others, the marriage partner in particular, when in houses three, six, and eleven, the characteristics of these houses would be stressed still more strongly.

This again raises the question of aspects. All aspects to Mercury influence the intellect, and while this is true for any planet in the sense that intellectual activity is affected by all other experiences in life, the aspects to Mercury are measured by the natures of the aspecting planets. Thus, a trine from Mars in Aquarius to Mercury in Libra in the second house would not have the same meaning if it were a trine from Saturn instead of Mars. Nor does a trine from Mars in Gemini to Mercury in Libra mean the same as one from Mars in Aquarius to Mercury in Libra.

With Mercury in the second house in Libra and Mars in the tenth house in Gemini, the native will gain through intellectual ability in a position of authority in his professional life whether as accountant, teacher, mathematician, surgeon, or butcher. But if Mars is in Libra in the sixth house, while financial gain is still possible, now the native will be in a subservient position, rendering service to others. While Mars in house six will bring out the native's mathematical abilities, this will be from an inferior social position, since house six is a cadent house as well as a weak one for Mars. Even so, other factors in the chart must be considered. Very prosperous physicians have been known with Mars in house six, and they have not always been surgeons.

Mercury rising ahead of the Sun has always been considered to benefit the intellect. It is said to be *casimi* when in the heart of the Sun, or within 30 minutes of longitude. In the author's opinion this is Mercury's strongest position as regards the effect of intellect on character because the individuality is more closely allied to intellect (the Sun, representing the ego, thus being the strongest influence on Mercury). But sign position must not be neglected and, if the Sun is afflicted with Mercury *casimi,* this will bring out the influence on character of the lowest phases of intellect.

Most astrologers agree that Mercury's weakest houses are five, eight, and twelve.

Mental defects or abnormalities are indicated not by Mercury alone but by serious afflictions of both Mercury and the Moon, as well as of the ruler of the third house, and by the malefics—Mars, Saturn, Uranus, Neptune, and Pluto. If the defect has a physical cause, the Moon's Nodes and the Ascendant may be involved.

Emotions

The emotional complexes in the horoscope are a more complicated matter upon which whole volumes could be written. Indeed, they are difficult for psychiatrists, psychologists, and psychoanalysts as well. Astrologically, the emotions are largely under the influence of Venus, the planet of feeling and affection; passion is shown by Mars; maternal affection by the Moon; paternal affection by the Sun; desire by Saturn; goodwill by Jupiter; fraternal feeling (or its absence) by Uranus; erotic feeling by Neptune; and spiritual introspection (or its opposite extreme) by Pluto.

Venus is a highly magnetic planet which is especially powerful on the Ascendant. Unless Mercury is extremely strong, an ascending Venus will cause feeling and emotions to play a more powerful role than intellect in the native's life.

While Venus is naturally very strong in Libra, Taurus, and Pisces, it is also highly sensitive to angular position. Also, as regards the emotions, Venus is especially significant in houses five and seven. Venus is very sensitive to aspects from Jupiter as well as being influenced strongly by the Sun and the Moon as it relates to ego and personality respectively.

Of particular interest in any chart is a sextile between Venus and Mercury, which the author believes to be the most beneficial aspect possible. Geometrically, this means only that both planets are close to their elongation from the Sun, which is thus located between them. Hence the emotions and intellect are balanced, which powerfully offsets what might otherwise be very detrimental to the native's character. When Venus rises ahead of the Sun and is sextile Mercury, feeling is somewhat stronger than intellect; conversely, if Mercury rises ahead of the Sun, the intellect predominates. In neither case, however, is the balance between emotions and intellect disturbed.

The student may now wish to analyze the influence of Venus on the emotions as Mercury's influence was analyzed on the intellect. This will be a very constructive exercise.

Action

Because of the relationship of Mars to passion we frequently regard it as the planet of emotion, but, strictly speaking, this is not quite true since Mars is fundamentally a planet of action. However, because of its strong relationship to the watery sign, Scorpio, its influence on the native's emotional character may be stronger than that of the other four positive celestial bodies: the Sun, Saturn, Uranus, and Pluto (depending on sign and house positions). Since antiquity Mars has been regarded as the ruler of Scorpio. The discovery of Pluto, and research on this planet to date, indicate strongly that Scorpio is its natural home or its sign of rulership. Therefore, Mars would be exalted in Scorpio.

The character is more strongly influenced by action (or what should more properly be called will-in-action) than by the intellect or the emotions. When any one of the five positive bodies is the strongest in a horoscope (and thus its ruler), the same domination of will-in-action will be found as when any combination of these bodies dominates the ascending sign or the Midheaven. Thus the Sun strengthens will-in-action because of its inbred authority and ability for leadership; Mars through its energy and activity as well as its too frequent pugnaciousness; Saturn through its ambition and latent force and its slow driving personality; Uranus through its controlled desire expressed aggressively but, too frequently, explosively; and Pluto through its steady and dominating desire to build anew on the experience of the past, changing while still clinging to the old.

Naturally these five bodies influence will-in-action, although positively, in widely different ways. A horoscope dominated by solar-martial influence will differ radically from one dominated by solar-saturnian influence. Other factors being equal, there will be as much action in one as in the other, but it may not appear on the surface of the character and will be expressed in a very different way. Here one must take fully into account the aspects, signs, and houses.

Synthesis

No horoscope is dominated completely by intellect, emotion, or will-in-action, since each chart is a synthesis of these three elements of character. Yet almost invariably one will be stronger than the other two, since man has not yet attained perfection. The combined influence of the three is tabulated in Table 7, which gives a keyword under each of the three elements of character thus expressing the quadruplicity or triplicity effect upon character, of intellect, emotion, or will-in-action. These, however, are only suggestions and the student's own experience will provide him with keys that better suit his manner of thinking.

Each of these three components is expressed through a combination of these quadruplicity-triplicity expressions. Thus the cardinal-earth combination expresses itself through intellect as an active-materialistic character; under emotion it would be

Table 7. Synthesis of Intellectual, Emotional, and Action Elements of Character.

Intellect	Emotion	Will-in-Action
Cardinal, Active	Cardinal, Creative	Cardinal, Aggressive
Fixed, Concentrative	Fixed, Faithful	Fixed, Conservative
Mutable, Versatile	Mutable, Harmonious	Mutable, Changeful
Earth, Material	Earth, Carnal	Earth, Possessive
Water, Romantic	Water, Emotional	Water, Expressive
Fire, Wilful	Fire, Ardent	Fire, Determination
Air, Intuitive	Air, Mystical	Air, Self-Development

creative-carnal nature; and under will-in-action, an inclusive possessive nature. Carrying the synthesis further, the dominating influences in the chart may be expressed through one celestial body in fixed-water as regards to intellect, while it may influence the emotional nature through another planet as cardinal-fire. Synthesis means developing a sufficiently broad perspective on the horoscope to grasp these combinations as a single unit.

A further factor must be included. The first house of the chart indicates personality, while the seventh house indicates the complement of the self or the partner (more broadly, the native's relationship to all others); the third house signifies the native's concrete practical sense and house nine (the complement of three) has to do with the abstract spiritual intelligence. When the rulers of the first and seventh houses are inharmonious with one another, the native has character or personality problems, sometimes inhibitions, which must be overcome. Similarly, conflict between houses three and nine creates internal character problems, internal conflicts. For a complete character synthesis all four of these houses must be analyzed.

Review Questions for Chapter 2

I. Find the hemisphere and quadrant balance in your own horoscope.

2. Are you more masculine or feminine? How does that help? Hinder?

3. Do your intellect, emotions, and manner of acting blend or conflict?

4. Combined with the essence or character determined in Chapter I how would you describe your basic character? In non-astrological terms now.

5. Do you see a connection between synthesis and Jungian psychology?

|Chapter 3|
Life Expectancy

Although more than 90 percent of an astrologer's clients are interested in one of the following three problems—position in life and finances, health, and emotional problems involving house five or seven—the competent practitioner must be able to assist with any problem of concern, thus synthesizing the horoscope should commence with factors which advance a knowledge of interpretation. As birth is the beginning of life in this world, and the horoscope is calculated for the time of birth, let us approach the subject from this same angle.

Infant Mortality

A newborn human infant is perhaps the most helpless creature in the world. Prior to birth its sustenance has been furnished through the medium of the mother, so only at birth does muscular development through respiration and assimilation of food begin in the child as a separate entity. At this point, survival is the most important question and, if casting the horoscope of a newborn babe, the first question to be answered is: what are the probabilities that he will survive infancy, childhood, and adolescence, reach maturity, middle age, or old age? The next question will be: to what diseases will the child be susceptible?" All subsequent horoscopic delineation will depend on the answers to these questions and many otherwise competent astrologers have badly failed in their prognostications of the future by failure to give adequate thought to the probably duration of life.

The practicing astrologer may be questioned by a parent concerning the child's vocational possibilities, and must be able to give answers which will not discredit astrology as a science and art.

The problems of life and death are entirely different and are determined by unique factors in the chart. Yet they are two parts of the same whole. Life is determined by a point on the horoscope called the Hyleg which, with very rare exceptions, is the Sun, the Moon, or the Ascendant. It is always the Sun when this body is in what is called a hylegiacal place. If it is not, and the Moon is in a hylegiacal place, then the Moon is the hyleg. If neither the Sun nor the Moon is in a hylegiacal place, then the Ascendant is the hyleg.

The hylegiacal places are:
1. The top half of the first house (Ascendant)
2. The top half of the eleventh house
3. The whole of the tenth house
4. The whole of the ninth house
5. The whole of the seventh house

In those rare instances when neither the Sun nor the Moon is in a hylegiacal place and the Ascendant is manifestly too weak to be strongly operative in the horoscope, the strongest planet found in a hylegiacal place is taken as the hyleg. This is indeed extremely rare.

When the hyleg has been ascertained, its strength or debility must be determined through its position, sign, quadruplicity, and triplicity. Then the nature of the aspects formed to the hyleg must be noted, with special attention to the planets forming these aspects. The Sun, the Moon, Jupiter, and Venus are aphetic bodies, meaning that they take away life. Mercury is either aphetic or anaretic, depending upon the planet which it translates. While the nature of aspects to the hyleg is important, an anaretic planet may prove anaretic even though aspecting the hyleg favorably and an aphetic planet may prove aphetic even though aspecting the hyleg unfavorably.

Thus it is well to prepare a list of good and bad aspects to the hyleg, to the Sun, the Moon, the Ascendant (one of these probably being the hyleg), and to the ruler of the horoscope (this being usually the ruler of the Ascendant, although it may also be the strongest planet in the chart).

Here is where the art of synthesis becomes important, as a conclusion cannot be reached through simple analysis, and one must have practice with actual charts preferably horoscopes of adults for whom the correct time of birth is known. The following must be noted:

1. Look for favorable aspects between the hyleg and the Moon (if the hyleg is the Sun or the Ascendant); between the hyleg and the Sun (if the hyleg is the Moon or the Ascendant); between Jupiter or Venus and the hyleg; or between Jupiter or Venus and the Sun, the Moon, the Ascendant, or the ruler of the horoscope. If one of these is present, there is a strong likelihood that the child will survive infancy. But it is also necessary to note whether the benefics are strong or weak by sign or house position and also whether they are posited in or have rulership over houses six, eight, or twelve. Obviously it is important to know if the planet is in the sign of its rulership, exaltation, debility, or fall, or is merely peregrine.

2. Look for aspects between the Sun and Mars plus, in a feminine chart, between the Moon and Mars. These give vitality but, if inharmonious, also denote fevers and accidents (the latter especially when Saturn or Uranus are involved). When Saturn is anaretic, benefic aspects of Saturn to the hyleg appear to be much less important in the early years of life than in the second half of life. Malefic aspects of Saturn to the hyleg, the Sun, or the Ascendant (if the Moon is hyleg) indicate a relatively weak

constitution during the formative years of life. However, Saturn's influence then appears to wane until the latter half of life, due largely to its association with crystallization processes and the nature of its influence, which is chronic. Chronic diseases are more likely to develop in persons who have reached maturity, although this is not invariable. Saturn, known to the ancient Greeks as Kronos, or time, is definitely associated with chronic ailments and accidents involving falls.

3. The influence of Mercury and Neptune are relevant. (Although some astrologers disregard these as important determinants of life or death, the author does not agree.) Mercury's nature must be carefully ascertained as well as that of the planet which it reflects or translates. Neptune is important in revealing influences which bring about death from obscure causes or from the native's habits. Neptune will have little influence on the early years of life unless strongly associated with house six, eighth, or twelve, or even house four.

4. The Moon, when it is not hyleg, is aphetic, more concerned with disease than with death unless it rules house four or eight. Its function as a minute hand of the clock of destiny is probably important, but otherwise (and especially in feminine charts) it is difficult to distinguish factors of life from factors of health and disease.

Understand that the signs of the zodiac are a means of indicating longitude along the ecliptic. The different sign positions indicate the geometrical angle between that point in the zodiac and the birth place and moment. The angles are expressed as though the signs confer different influences or powers (planes of action) in relationship to the Ascendant. For convenience this is expressed as though the signs themselves had power or influence over the Ascendant and, to a lesser degree, the same type of influence when containing either the Sun or the Moon. In respect of the factors of life they are:

- Vital Signs: Aries, Leo, Libra, and Sagittarius
- Enduring Signs: Gemini and Virgo
- Advancing Signs: (weak in infancy but stronger later in life): Capricorn, Taurus, and Scorpio
- Frail Sign: Aquarius
- Weak Signs: Cancer and Pisces

Thus, not only must the good and bad aspects to the hyleg, the other luminary, the Ascendant, and the ruler of the chart be balanced; but the signs in which the first three are placed must be taken into consideration, the relations (if any) between them and houses six, eight, or twelve must be ascertained, plus define the strength or debility of the bodies in question.

Most astrologers regard the following serious afflictions as likely to indicate death in infancy:

1. All four factors (Sun, Moon, Ascendant, and ruler) afflicted without helpful aspects from Jupiter or Venus.

2. The Sun, Moon, and ruler in menacing houses (six, eighth, or twelve) or, together with the Ascendant, in weak signs.

3. The horoscope ruler in house eight with malefics in the Ascendant or throwing malefic aspects to the hyleg. (However, the author accepts this only if the ruler is debilitated in house eight.)

4. The Sun, Moon, and a malefic in trine relationship to one another (grand trine) without strong help from the benefics. (However, the author does not accept this view and has many charts which disprove it.)

5. The Sun and Moon in opposition to one another (Full Moon) and square to malefics which are in conjunction, which generally indicates a stillborn child.

6. Birth at the moment of an eclipse, especially if the malefics throw aspects to the point.

It has been asserted that an infant cannot survive birth if Saturn is posited precisely on his Ascendant, but this is not true. Saturn on the Ascendant indicates difficulty in starting to breathe and danger of smothering (a Saturn attribute); hence such births are so-called blue babies. For death to occur at birth the hyleg must be afflicted. It is an astrological aphorism that death occurs only at a time when the hyleg is afflicted. Hence there is grave danger of loss of the child if the Ascendant afflicted by Saturn is the hyleg.

Mars conjunction any of the four angles (cusps of houses one, four, seven, and ten) or strongly aspecting the Sun in these positions often indicates a caesarean birth. Neptune in these positions indicates birth under peculiar circumstances, ranging from illegitimacy to breach birth. Other factors must be investigated, and the charts of the parents may also have to be consulted.

End of Life

Most of the foregoing indications have been presented as sources of denial of life in the chart and are essentially factors affecting the child's vitality. In passing to the question of death later in life, the student should be warned in general against stipulating what seems to him to be the *terminus vitae* in the chart. This is done only under the most unusual circumstances and upon written request by the native. Such exceptional circumstances may include collaboration of the astrologer with a licensed physician or practitioner of the healing art who may desire this information.

There are many reasons for the above admonition, only one or two of which need be mentioned here. First, no sincere astrologer will ever make absolutely precise predictions with respect to any individual, as this implies irrevocability of fate and the absence of choice by the individual. Astrology merely indicates the influences which seem to be operating at a given time. Foreknowledge of their nature and time of operation is an instrument for combating them. Second, the astrologer is only human and thus subject to human limitations. He can, and does overlook some of the complex factors operating in the horoscope. Death is not usually indicated by any single configuration but is the climax of a running series of malefic combinations. Finally, the astrologer must beware of the psychological effect that such a delineation might have upon the client.

However, these reasons should not prevent an astrologer from applying general rules to measure the approximate life expectancy as this is necessary for his own guidance. In this connection, the author rarely gives detailed advice on the horoscope for more than one year in advance. Environmental conditions, often difficult to analyze astrologically, may change radically, and these will have an effect on the interpretation.

As has been discussed earlier, house eight indicates death and matters relating to the dead, while house four indicates the environment of old age and the end of life. Thus, the rulers of these houses and the planets in them must be noted. Death cannot be foretold precisely from any natal chart; even in the progressed horoscope the nature of the directions must be studied carefully.

However, the natal chart, especially in certain types of configurations, usually indicates the manner in which death occurs, although hard and fast rules for this cannot be laid down. In astrology, as in medicine, law, or art, rules are designed merely to direct thinking into certain broad channels, so in the final analysis the guide must be practice or clinical experience.

With this admonition the following clues are presented, but the manner of death is so closely related to pathological astrology that more specific information on this would require a complete course of instruction in the latter discipline.

Eighth House Cusp Signs

Generally speaking, therefore, the sign on the eighth house cusp indicates the following:

Aries on cusp eight means death is often the result of the native's own actions.

Taurus on cusp eight means danger of death from personal excesses or chronic ailments; this sign is particularly unfavorable for surgical operations.

Gemini on cusp eight means death through a respiratory ailment or through complications of another disease; many astrologers regard as unfavorable here the influence of a relative of the native.

Cancer on cusp eight means death is usually through functional disease or by drowning; often it is threatened before its actual occurrence.

Leo on cusp eight means death is sudden and from natural causes, often heart disease.

Virgo on cusp eight means intestinal ailments are often a contributing cause, but death is usually quiet and peaceful.

Libra on cusp eight means kidney difficulties often help bring on death, with inability to excrete or eliminate poisons from the system; death usually comes in circumstances of stress and worry.

Scorpio on cusp eight means there is a liability to a mysterious, sudden, and violent end; death may also be due to a disease of the procreative organs.

Sagittarius on cusp eight means a peaceful and happy death in agreeable surroundings.

Capricorn on cusp eight means death generally results from complications of chronic ailments, with the native in a depressed state of mind.

Aquarius on cusp eight often indicates death through accident or acute infection; *it* may sometimes come abut through mental shock.

Pisces on cusp eight means death often comes *in* an obscure manner, through a long-standing or psychic disease; the physician will have difficulty diagnosing the cause of death.

Planets in the Eighth House

When the celestial bodies are posited in the eighth house or rule it, the following indications are obtained:

Sun in eighth house: Well-aspected means death through hereditary weakness or heart trouble in a public place or before the public in some way; there is a suggestion of posthumous honors. Afflicted means there is sudden or violent death in middle age.

Moon in eighth house: Well-aspected means death through functional causes; frequently in a hospital, a public place, or in the presence of strangers (especially if the twelfth house is involved. Afflicted means death in public or a tragic death, as by drowning; death through a respiratory disease (note Mars position also).

Mercury in eighth house: Well-aspected means death through a mental or nervous disease, usually as the result of complications; the native is often conscious at the moment of death. Afflicted means the native is in terror of death; there is delirium just before death and, in some cases, incipient insanity.

Venus in eighth house: Well-aspected means a peaceful death in excellent surroundings. Afflicted means death through a wasting disease; may be due to personal excesses but note the sign and the nature of the aspects.

Mars in eighth house: Well-aspected means death is sudden and often violent; may be due to personal excesses (note house rulership of Mars). Afflicted means death almost always is sudden and violent, and sometimes the consequence of violence on the native's part.

Jupiter in eighth house: Well-aspected means a peaceful end with the best religious and medical ministrations. Afflicted means death from tumors, growths, or slowly developing diseases; medical care and nursing are unsatisfactory.

Saturn in eighth house: Well-aspected means death from chronic ailment but with sufficient time for preparation; the faculties are active to the end. Afflicted means death is painful and follows upon a lingering illness; persons around the native are often selfish or treacherous.

Uranus in eighth house: Well-aspected means sudden and unexpected death from accident, explosion, lightning, or violence. Afflicted means death is preceded by paralysis and there are unusual or painful contractions or mutilations of the body.

Neptune in eighth house: Well-aspected means death is in some way strange, unusual, or chaotic, surrounded by mystery; correct diagnosis may be impossible. Afflicted means native may be a drug addict; poison or drugs may be administered incorrectly; death may come while native is in a trance or insane; prior to modern methods of burial, there was great danger of being buried alive.

Pluto in eighth house: Well-aspected means that though death be from natural causes there may be a need for an inquest or post mortem. Death could be from excessive radiation; result of heroic action, mine cave-in; or paralysis. Afflicted means disappearing without a trace of the physical body even being found; blood poisoning; or bombing victim.

This list is only suggestive. The student cannot be warned too frequently to determine all of the factors in the horoscope and then synthesize them. No single portion of the horoscope can be considered in isolation, as life itself is a whole. Any death from illness, in particular, must be due to a combination of factors. A single aspect, or limited number of aspects, are involved only in sudden death from external causes.

An insight into the correct method of synthesizing can be obtained from our statement above concerning death when Aries is on the eighth house cusp: "death is often the result of the native's own actions." If Venus and Saturn are strong in the horoscope and afflicted, suicidal tendencies are indicated; likewise if the ruler of house eight is in house one and seriously afflicted. Also, suicide is possible when there is an Aries influence in house eight, and the ruler of the Ascendant is involved in the affliction of Venus and Saturn. If the Moon is afflicted with Aries on the house eight cusp, especially if Neptune and house eight are involved, death by suffocation is indicated (drowning, gassing, etc.) just as when Pisces is unfortunate in the chart. With Aries on the eighth house cusp and Jupiter strong, especially with Mars or Pluto prominent (making the native reckless and imprudent), death may come about through some heroic act for reasons of honor or through recklessness where the native throws discretion to the winds.

All of the foregoing are probabilities indicated by the natal chart, but death indications are also found by progressing the horoscope. The manner of death is determined largely by the native's environment: hence the importance of the progressed chart which indicates the native's progression through life. Many aphorisms have been handed down from ancient times concerning the nature of the different kinds of death. While civilization has advanced, and the manner of death has changed (in the United States we do not expect such ancient or medieval types of death as hanging, poisoning, burning at the stake, stabbing in the back, or starvation in prison, which were formerly more or less common), the principles still stand. They are as valid today as in the times of Ptolemy, Trismegistus, or the Chaldeans but must be interpreted in terms of the twentieth century not of the first or fifteenth century The student will find it easy to remain true to these principles by remembering that a horoscope is not a case but the picture of an actual man or woman.

Review Questions for Chapter 3

1. Locate the hyleg in your horoscope. List the possible hylegiacal places.

2. What is the relevancy of determining life expectancy?

3. How is house eight connected with the end of life?

4. List the factors of life for each zodiac sign.

5. What causes "blue babies"?

|Chapter 4|

Health Indicators

The subject of health and disease in astrology could hardly be covered even in a course of average length, and a single chapter can only touch the highlights. Furthermore, this topic will be difficult for anyone to understand who has not already been trained in one of the healing sciences or physiology, pathology, or therapeutics.

Volumes I and II of this textbook series gave some information on physiological or pathological astrology, particularly as regards the signs and the planets. After completing this study and acquiring some practice in applying its principles, the student should have sufficient working knowledge to cooperate with practitioners of the healing arts. He will at least be able to cover the subject when casting a horoscope, although specialization would require a much more comprehensive study.

The first house relates to health and the sixth to disease, but in a broader sense the whole chart must always be considered, since no part of the body is isolated from the rest. Health is very different from disease: the former is constructive, promotes growth, and stimulates the development of personality and character, while the latter is destructive and retards or blocks growth, personality, and character.

Afflictions in Health

While the hyleg is of secondary importance, careful attention must be paid to it since afflictions of the Sun, Moon, Ascendant, or ruler of the horoscope will necessarily be more critical (other factors being equal) than afflictions of any other point on the chart.

The considerations outlined in connection with the other phases of life's expression must always be borne in mind, and the student is again reminded of them:

1. Afflictions from malefics are more dangerous than those from benefics.

2. Afflictions from planets in weak signs are more dangerous than from those in strong or vital signs.

3. Afflictions from houses four, six, eight, or twelve or from the rulers of these houses, are more serious than from other houses.

4. Malefics in exaltation or in dignity are less serious than in detriment or fall.

5. The affliction may affect the part of the body ruled by the indicated sign (Table 8), by the house occupied, or by the planet itself (the same is true for any other subject in astrology). This is a rather difficult point and requires some practice in interpretation. Thus it should be explained in more detail.

Any affliction involves six possible considerations:
a. the sign of the afflicted planet,
b. the house of the afflicted planet,
c. the afflicted planet or luminary itself,
d. the sign of the afflicting planet,
e. the house of the afflicting planet, and
f. the afflicting planet or luminary itself.

Table 8. Human Body and the Zodiac.	
Zodiac Sign	*Body Area*
Aries	Head
Taurus	Throat and Neck
Gemini	Shoulders and Arms
Cancer	Breasts and Stomach
Leo	Heart, Spine, and Back
Virgo	Intestines
Libra	Kidneys
Scorpio	Sex Organs
Sagittarius	Hips and Thighs
Capricorn	Knees, Bones, and Teeth
Aquarius	Circulation
Pisces	Feet

Hence any affliction may give rise to one or more of six possible delineations, and without practice the student will have difficulty in settling on the correct one. Accuracy and ability are developed only through practice.

The first step is to determine which of these six points is otherwise afflicted in the horoscope, for the physical disability resulting from several afflictions will probably be more severe. Thus, the head is governed by the Ascendant and also by Aries (ruled by Mars). The Moon governs the blood and other bodily fluids. Jupiter rules the arterial system. The Sun governs the heart. Capricorn governs the skeleton generally and the legs specifically, from a point about midway between the hip and the knee to one about midway between the knees and the ankles.

With all of this in mind, let us suppose that in a natal chart Mars and the Moon are conjunct in Aries in the first house in square aspect with the Sun in Capricorn. The Moon will pass over the natal Sun by secondary progression (discussed in Volume IV) in the native's forty-eighth to fiftieth year. Assume that transiting Jupiter is conjunct the Sun at the same time. With all of these factors present one would expect the Mars-Moon affliction in Aries to bring on liability to an accident in the thigh or leg with hemorrhage. The Sun in Capricorn will not indicate the affliction because only one factor in the natal chart affects the Sun, while there are four factors affecting the Aries configuration of Mars-Moon. Since Jupiter square Mars tends to increase the blood pressure, there is danger of cerebral hemorrhage at that age in life, and the astrologer should warn his client in advance to see his physician and take the necessary protective measures.

In physiological astrology precedence is accorded to the sign rather than the house. Thus, while house five indicates the heart physiologically (the houses having the same meanings as the corresponding signs, in numerical rotation), the sign Leo would be more indicative of the heart in whatever house it is found. Likewise, the sign usually indicates the part of the body affected, and the planet tells the general type of disease attacking that part of the body. Recent research, however, suggests that the mundane or precise house position is very important. And the aspects between the planets, the Ascendant, and the Midheaven are of significance.

The planets also have special attributes:

Sun—vital

Moon—nutritive

Mercury—assuming nature of body influencing it most strongly

Mars—inflammatory or heating

Jupiter—plethoric (blood conditions usually involving an excess of blood)

Saturn—chronic

Uranus—spasmodic

Neptune—comatose

Pluto—environmental or congenital

The Sun, Mars, Jupiter, Uranus and Pluto are tonic (they impart vital energy), positive, and electric. The Moon, Saturn, Venus, and Neptune are atonic (wanting in vital energy), negative, and magnetic. Mercury, again, depends on its strongest aspect.

Triplicities in Health

Another important consideration is the triplicities. Since these are basic to all charts, many astrologers start their delineations here. Allied with this division of the triplicities is that of the four basic temperaments, which are given in order to show their relationships to the planets as well as to the triplicities.

Fire Signs

The fiery signs are associated with the vital heat and with all that is connected with the action of mind and will over matter.

In the bilious temperament the nutritive system predominates. It is usually characterized by a dark complexion, muscular activity, energy, firmness of purpose, and a passionate disposition. It is sometimes called the choleric temperament and is related to the fiery triplicity by the planet Mars as well as by the Sun (when in certain signs—usually all except Aries, Leo, and Sagittarius).

Earth Signs

The earthy signs are associated with the bones, tendons, ligaments, and the mineral basis of the human system.

The sanguine temperament is marked by rugged and enduring physical vitality but is liable to nervous exhaustion. The native is frequently melancholic, brooding, and irritable. The body is solid and compact, and the complexion varies. This temperament is related to the earthy triplicity, the planet Jupiter, and the Sun in Aries, Leo, and Sagittarius.

Air Signs

The airy signs are associated with the gases, intercellular space, arteries, veins, and capillaries.

In the Nervous Temperament, as the name implies, the nervous organization is exceedingly sensitive. These persons are usually thin and wiry, of medium complexion, and mentally and physically quick. It is related to the airy triplicity by Mercury and Uranus as well as by Saturn (except when it is in watery signs).

Water Signs

The watery signs are related to the body's fluids. The manner of death is an excellent example of how each sign in the triplicity has its particular function while sharing in the fundamental character of the triplicity. For example, Cancer governs the milk, the digestive juices (saliva, gastric juice, and pancreatic juice), and the chyme. Scorpio governs the excrementitious fluids: urine, perspiration, and menstrual blood. Pisces governs the sera and fluids of the body's mucous membranes.

In the lymphatic temperament the lymphatic system predominates, and the native is flabby, usually of pale complexion, heavy, and passionless. This is sometimes called the phlegmatic temperament and is related to the watery triplicity, the Moon, Venus, Neptune, and Pluto, as well as to Saturn in the water signs, particularly Pisces or Cancer.

Quadruplicities in Health

The quadruplicities are of much less importance in diagnosis but seem to be more important (with respect to timing) in prognosis. The cardinal quadruplicity has more to do with acute ailments, those which come and go quickly. The fixed quadruplicity has more to do with chronic ailments, illnesses of longer duration. The mutable quadruplicity relates to superficial illnesses. These, however, should not be confused with timing in disease which is quite another matter, related primarily to the Sun and Moon.

The planets and luminaries are related to disease in the following way:

Sun—hot and dry

Moon—cold and moist

Mercury—convertible according to aspect

Venus—warm and moist

Mars—hot and dry

Jupiter—hot and moist

Saturn—cold and dry

Uranus—cold and dry (Although there is much disagreement here, because the explosive nature of Uranus does not suggest cold. In its gaseous nature it is probably cold, but in its electric nature it is hot.)

Neptune—warm and moist

Pluto—hot and moist

This list indicates the nature of certain aspects in a given sign and house. Thus, the Moon and Mars are eruptive and contradictory. Venus and Neptune are in sympathy with one another (Neptune is a higher octave of the vibrations of Venus), both being warm and moist. Mars and Jupiter tend to obesity, and in some aspects this is probably due to the deficiency in iron which they indicate. Mars and Saturn are contradictory; their mutual antipathy causes waste of tissue, hence thinness.

Planets in Health

The student will now understand why physiological astrology demands some knowledge of physiology and pathology. He must know the parts of the body ruled by the various signs and the diseases characteristic of the various planets; then he must apply these to the other different factors given above. In this connection the following method has been found useful:

1. Determine the native's temperament, its strengths and weaknesses. An individual will rarely be found who is clearly of a single type, as two or more temperaments are almost always blended. The strongest is important for the native's positive features, the weakest for his negative ones.

2. Determine the hyleg.

3. Consider the strengths and weaknesses of the Sun, Moon, Ascendant, and ruler of the chart, determining whether they are strong or weak by sign and house.

4. Prepare a list of aspects for the Sun, Moon, Ascendant, and ruler of the horoscope, determining whether the preponderance is for good or ill. Consider bad aspects (especially oppositions, squares, and conjunctions with malefics) as catabolic or destructive and good aspects (especially trines, sextiles, and conjunctions with benefics) as anabolic or constructive. Place the Sun, Moon, Ascendant, and ruler of the horoscope in a widely spaced column down the middle of a page, drawing slanting lines to the right to list catabolic (malefic) aspects and slanting lines to the left to list anabolic (benefic) aspects. This will reveal at a glance the balance of forces, indicating whether the destructive forces are heavily loaded with aspects from malefics.

5. Analyze the Sun, Moon, Ascendant, and ruler of the chart, and then synthesize them. This information, added to the analysis of the temperament, should give the main groundwork for diagnosis.

6. The next step is to account for the malefics (Mars and Saturn) and the semi-malefics (Uranus, Neptune, and Pluto). Since the former are malefic (in physiological astrology), their mere presence in the horoscope is a menace. The points they occupy are points of menace. The points they occupy are points of menace and should be noted as kinetic (potential) danger points. The following list may be of service.

Mars in Health Places

Mars in Aries gives pains in head; cerebral congestion; insomnia; smallpox; and delirium.

Mars in Taurus gives laryngitis; tonsillitis; colds with fever; adenoid troubles; diphtheria; and diseases of the upper bronchi (if in last degrees of Taurus).

Mars in Gemini gives bronchitis; pneumonia; inflammations of the lungs; injuries of the collarbone, arms, or hands; and nervous diseases.

Mars in Cancer gives hemorrhage of the stomach (ulcers); gastritis; nausea; coughs; inflammations of the breasts; and hepatic (liver) ailments affecting the digestion.

Mars in Leo gives heart disease; angina; sunstroke; herpes (affections of the skin or mucous surfaces); zoster or zona (acute inflammatory disease characterized by groups of small vesicles on an inflammatory base and associated with neuralgic pain; and aneurisms (dilations of the arteries).

Mars in Virgo gives inflammations of the bowels (enteritis); cholera; appendicitis; hernia; and typhoid fever.

Mars in Libra gives nephritis (inflammation of the kidneys); pyelitis (inflammation of the pelvis of the kidney); severe back pains; and occasionally appendicitis (the latter appears to be also related to Virgo, Leo, and Scorpio).

Mars in Scorpio gives bladder inflammations; hernias; inflammations of the genitals; menorrhagia (excessive menstrual flow); scarlatina; prostatitis; urethritis; and gonorrhea.

Mars in Sagittarius gives acute sciatica; ulcers of the hips and thighs; enteric fever (typhoid); and occasionally hemorrhoids (these belong more properly to Scorpio).

Mars in Capricorn gives rheumatic fever (a viral disease, not to be confused with rheumatism); smallpox; urticaria (an inflammatory disease producing itching wheals on the skin); anthrax; gout; and various skin eruptions, particularly if Mercury is involved.

Mars in Aquarius give intermittent fevers; blood poisoning; erysipelas (acute spreading inflammation of the skin and subcutaneous tissue); and overheated blood.

Mars in Pisces given bunions; corns; excessive perspiration of the feet; sometimes gout (also with Capricorn); and chronic alcoholism, leading to *delirium tremens*.

Saturn in Health Places

When Saturn is contrasted with these martian influences in the signs, the student will have a correct insight into the correct presentation of the planets in all signs in physiological astrology. It must be recalled that Mars is hot and dry, Saturn is cold and dry, Mars is acute, Saturn is chronic. The elements of coldness and chronicity are shown strongly in the following listing

Saturn in Aries gives catarrh; deafness; toothache, chill; cerebral anemia; apathy; and paralysis.

Saturn in Taurus gives laryngeal consumption; spitting coughs; coryza (inflammation of mucous membranes of the eyes); colds; aphonia (loss of speech); gangrene; and relaxations of the throat.

Saturn in Gemini gives tuberculosis; fibrosis (degeneration of the lung tissue); dyspnea (difficult or labored breathing); jaundice (changes in the liver cells preventing them from retaining their secretions; they are diffused into the blood and cause the skin and whites of the eyes to be yellow); plus rheumatism of the arms and shoulders.

Saturn in Cancer gives asthma; ague; dyspepsia; chronic gastritis; cancer of the breasts and axillae; eructations (belching); and chlorosis (perverted biliary secretion).

Saturn in Leo gives weak heart; valvular insufficiency; atrophy; weakness of the back; and locomotor ataxia (inability to coordinate the action of the voluntary muscles).

Saturn in Virgo gives malnutrition; rickets; sluggishness of the liver; insufficient peristalsis of the intestinal tract; abdominal phthisis (tuberculosis); chronic appendicitis; and constipation.

Saturn in Libra gives Bright's disease; renal colic; painful sterility; suppression of urine; and impurity of blood due to kidney failure.

Saturn in Scorpio gives retention of urine; fistula; gravel or stone; and insufficient menstrual flow.

Saturn in Sagittarius gives slow gout; tuberculosis of the hip; and pelvic pains upon standing.

Saturn in Capricorn gives chronic articular rheumatism; skin diseases; and synovitis (inflammation of the membranes which line the joints).

Saturn in Aquarius gives curvature of the spine; caries (inflammation of the bone) of the spine; anemia; cramps; weak and sprained ankles; arteriosclerosis (abnormal thickening or hardening of the arterial wall); plus varicose veins.

Saturn in Pisces gives ulcers of the feet; chilblains; scrofula (glandular swelling of the neck combined with inflammation of the joints and mucous membranes); plus pains in the feet allied to pains in the head.

Uranus in Health Places

Uranus in all signs means sudden attacks of disease; cramps; spasms; shocks; exaggerated pains; plus spasmodic attacks of nerves.

Neptune in Health Places

Neptune in all signs gives obscure and psychic diseases; as well as internal and external poisonings of all kinds.

Pluto in Health Places

Pluto in all signs brings on hallucinations during fevers; inflammation of nerve ganglia; shock; radiation sickness; hypochondria; psychological disturbances; and abscesses.

7. When the static points of the malefics have been determined, the evil aspects from these points must be listed. Here it must be remembered that attention focuses on the signs. Thus, if Mars is in Leo squared by Mercury in Scorpio, Mars is not throwing kinetic energy upon Mercury, but Leo is doing this to Scorpio. For the sake of thoroughness, it is advisable to make a second chart or table with Mars, Saturn, Uranus, and Neptune on the left side of the page; then draw as many lines as necessary from the static sign in which the malefic is located to the signs which are brought into play by the malefic kinetic ray.

8. The following suggestive rules for the ruler of house six are given in Vivian Robson's *A Student's Textbook of Astrology*. These deal only with an afflicted ruler of the sixth house:

Ruler of the sixth house in the first gives ill health due to the fault of the native.

Ruler of the sixth house in the second gives loss of money through expenditures on sickness.

Ruler of the sixth house in the third gives illnesses on journeys.

Ruler of the sixth house in the fourth gives hereditary illnesses.

Ruler of the sixth house in the fifth gives illness due to pleasures.

Ruler of the sixth house in the sixth gives occupational diseases and illnesses from overwork.

Ruler of the sixth house in the seventh gives illnesses through marriage or through infection by a woman as well as epidemic diseases (lack of receptivity to inoculations).

Ruler of the sixth house in the eighth gives poor health generally; the native is frequently at the door of death.

Ruler of the sixth house in the ninth gives illnesses abroad or at a distance from home plus mania.

Ruler of the sixth house in the tenth gives illnesses due to business affairs or to excessive responsibility on the native.

Ruler of the sixth in the eleventh house gives illnesses due to worries and disappointments.

Ruler of the sixth house in the twelfth gives illnesses requiring a stay in hospital or asylum.

There are special rules for particular diseases and types of accidents, but these are too lengthy for presentation in a single chapter. The therapeutics of physiological astrology is also a special subject, with every chemical property classified under its zodiacal sign and every element (and most of the compounds) classified under its own ruler, luminary, or planet.[4] When the horoscope is known, and its weaknesses are revealed, astrological therapeutics endeavors to supply correctives to the native for his deficiencies, thus to establish a balance in the body permitting nature to bring about the cure. However, it does not attempt to supplant academic medicine. Rather, many physicians use astrology for assistance in diagnosis and prognosis.

As a supplement to this lesson the student may wish to consult various other medical references.[5]

Review Questions for Chapter 4

1. What potential illnesses are shown in your own horoscope by the sign and house position of the greater and lesser malefics?

2. Which houses indicate good or poor health and what is the basic difference?

3. What are the attributes and temperaments of the planets as related to health factors?

4. Name the four basic temperaments and show how they are associated to astrology's elements of fire, earth, air, and water.

5. Show the body portions ruled by each zodiac sign.

| Chapter 5 |

Family Relationships

One of the most difficult yet most frequent problems facing any individual is that of relating with other people. The fundamental framework for interrelating is established during childhood by the examples of parents, siblings, grandparents, and other relatives. Just as the home environment expands in later life into the cooperation or conflicts of the native's world, so do these early patterns become the model from which the native bases his or her understanding of others.

Relationship problems occur in all phases of human existence from international trade to political campaigns to romantic endeavors. Every stage of life is spent in contact with peers, superiors, and inferiors from student and teacher, through manager and employee.

The initial attempt to understand how a native communicates and relates with another individual is to thoroughly comprehend the early patterns of relationship within the family unit. This can best be accomplished by synthesizing the horoscope factors that deal with parental influence, brother and sister love or rivalry, blood relative ties, and the home environment.

Parents

Houses four and 10 represent the native's parents. However, astrologers do not agree which house represents the father and which the mother. As mentioned in Chapter 1, the best rule is to consider house four as indicating the parent of the opposite sex, unless Cancer be on the cusp, which would always represent the mother. Similarly, the tenth house cusp must be considered to indicate the parent of the same sex unless Leo be found in it, in which case it always represents the father. Contrariwise, Leo on the fourth house cusp always indicates the father, and Cancer on the tenth always indicates the mother.

Our experience shows this to be a better rule than the other (advocated by many astrologers), that the fourth always represents the father and the tenth always is the mother. But even this rule *does* not hold true always, being most often correct when the native is the eldest child. Still, it is more reliable than any other rule that has come to the author's attention.

Thus, it is often difficult to decide which house represents which parent, and careful synthesis is needed. With this rule in mind, some of the other factors to be considered in doubtful cases are as follows:

1. If the parents' birth dates and times are known, note the sign and house positions of the rulers of houses four and 10 of the native's chart, or the planets in these houses, and decide if there is any connection with the parent's charts. In a male chart, for example, assume that Taurus is on the fourth house cusp and Venus, its ruler, is in Aries; note whether either parent has the Sun in Aries, has Aries ascending, or has Aries on the fifth house cusp (children). This may be suggestive.

2. If a physical description of the parents is available, note which of the two cusps (together with their rulers and the latter's positions) most accurately describes each of the two parents.

3. If a feminine sign is on the fourth house, and its ruler is in a feminine sign, this may suggest the mother; if a masculine sign is found here, and its ruler is in a masculine sign, this may suggest the father.

The Sun has always signified fatherhood, and the Moon motherhood. In these broad general senses, therefore, the Sun and Moon indicate the native's father and mother. Similarly, Saturn is paternal and Venus maternal, but in a somewhat more personal sense. However, the Sun, Moon, Saturn, and Venus, together with the Ascendant, are more indicative of heredity on either the paternal or maternal side of the family. If Venus and Saturn are both in masculine signs, greater hereditary influence from the father's side is indicated; if both are in feminine signs, the greater hereditary influence is from the mother. If one is in a masculine sign and the other in a feminine sign, hereditary influences from both sides of the family are indicated. If both planets are in masculine signs, the father's influence on the native will probably be greater than the mother's; if both are in feminine signs, the mother's influence will be greater than the father's. If divided, neither parent will greatly influence the native unless the ruler of the Ascendant is in close favorable aspect with the ruler of either the fourth or tenth house, in which case the parent so represented will be closer to the native. These factors affect the native psychologically as well as physiologically.

The next stage of synthesis requires applying the same principles to the Sun and the Moon, but with one small difference: if the Sun and Moon are both in masculine signs, hereditary influence is chiefly through the father; if both are in feminine signs, the mother is the principal influence on the children's heredity; if the Sun is in a masculine sign and the Moon in a feminine sign, the influence is about equally divided between father and mother; but if the Sun is in a feminine sign, and the Moon in a masculine sign, heredity plays little part in the determination of character or physical appearance.

Most Western astrologers regard house four as indicating the father, but oriental astrologers regard house four as always indicating the mother. In either method, the opposite house represents the other parent.

The relationships between the rulers of houses four and 10, as well as the relationships or polarities between the Sun and the Moon, reveal much information about the native's character. If the rulers of houses four and 10 afflict one another, the life of the parents (and thus the home life in childhood) was probably inharmonious. Whatever difficulties are indicated will influence the native for good or ill, and if the Sun and Moon are also not in harmony with one another, the native will definitely be under a powerful disadvantage. For instance, if the Sun and Moon are square each other, the native is restless, nervous, and easily upset. If the rulers of houses four and 10 also afflict one another, this condition affects the childhood environment (other environmental influences are discussed later in this chapter).

If the Sun is favorably aspected and the Moon is unfavorably aspected, many astrologers hold that the father will outlive the mother. In our opinion, however, this is true only if one of these planets rules or is posited in either house four or 10. While planetary positions may be read in many different ways, plausibility should not be mistaken for logic and reason.

If the ruler of either of these houses is in the Ascendant and well aspected, the parent thus represented will have a strong influence on the native. If badly aspected, there will be a clash of personality between the native and this parent. If the ruler of the Ascendant afflicts the rulers of either house four or 10, there will be a clash between the native and that parent.

The general principles of astrology should be applied down the line in direct relationship to the parents, and then given specific interpretation.

Brothers and Sisters

Brothers and sisters are represented by house three, but synthesis of the horoscope must proceed a step further. Indeed, this same step further should be taken in all astrological determination of personal relationships.

The Ascendant relates to the native and its complement, house seven, has a direct impact on the native's attitude toward, and relationship with, all other persons. Thus, house seven is not dedicated solely to contracts and marriage. The native whose houses three and seven are harmonious is much more likely to have harmonious relationships with brothers and sisters, as well as parents, aunts, uncles, friends, and all other persons than the person with an afflicted house seven.

The sign Gemini also has much to do with brothers and sisters. Persons with many planets in the third house or in Gemini, and well-aspected, are very clannish in their family relationships. If afflicted in these positions, brothers or sisters may cause family difficulties.

Uranus, Saturn, or Neptune in the third house or ruling the third, particularly if afflicted, often deny brothers and sisters plus indicate that the native is an only child. If affliction is by the ruler of house eight, or if these planets are in the eighth and afflicted, death of a brother or sister may be indicated.

Some astrologers have held house that the third house indicates the native's eldest brother or sister, or the one next older than himself; thus house five the next, house nine the next, and so on. This is an interesting thesis, but too much credence should not be placed in it. While it may be tested experimentally, to date no positive rule has emerged.

Other Relatives

Following the principles of horary astrology, relatives may be determined by the relationship of the various houses to houses four and 10. Thus, houses six and 12 (which are the third houses from the fourth and tenth, the brothers and sisters of the parents) would indicate the native's aunts and uncles. Houses one and seven (which are the fourth houses from the fourth and tenth) would represent the grandparents. Similarly, the brothers and sisters of the marriage partner would be indicated by house nine (which is the third from the seventh), while the parents-in-law would be represented by the houses opposite those of the native's parents, i.e., if the fourth represents the mother, it also represents the father-in-law (being the fourth from house seven.

Figure 3, Houses Showing Various Relatives

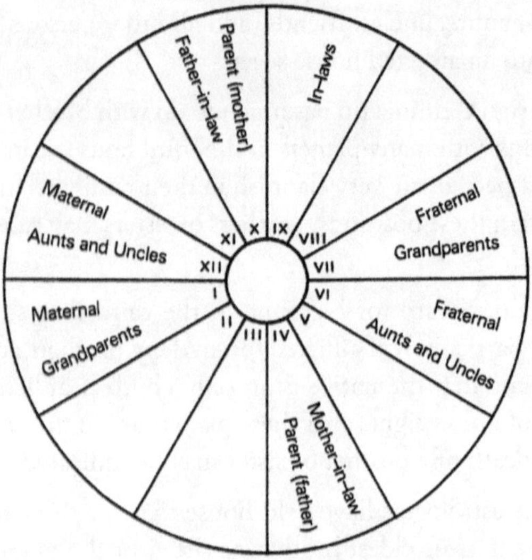

[Figure 3: A circular chart divided into twelve houses showing: Parent (mother)/Father-in-law (X), In-laws (IX), Fraternal Grandparents (VIII), (VII), Fraternal Aunts and Uncles (VI), Mother-in-law/Parent (father) (IV), (III), Maternal Grandparents (II), (I), Maternal Aunts and Uncles (XII), (XI), (V)]

Mercury, Venus, and Mars rule male and female relatives of the native's own generation; Jupiter rules aunts and uncles; Saturn, Uranus, Neptune, and Pluto rule the grandparents and other relatives of that generation. Care must be exercised here, however, for only those individuals are indicated whose lives are connected personally with that of the native. Astrology deals with the effects of cosmic influences as they relate to the native himself.

Home Environment

House four is usually called the house of environment, but, strictly speaking, the entire horoscope deals with environment: house six is the environment of employment, house seven the environment of personal relations with others, etc. And certainly the influence of brothers and sisters upon the native's childhood will greatly affect his start in life. But it is also true that the home environment, house four, has a more dominant influence on the native than any of these others.

Yet astrology disproves the adage that, "We are victims of our environment," and provides a new one: "We are the creators of our environment." The native is responsible for creating that environment through his character which will afford him the greatest opportunity in life.

Thus, it is the astrologer's duty to determine the astrological harmony of the horoscope. On this more extended instruction is furnished later, but in connection with the determination of environment it will be revealed by an inharmonious horoscope. This does not necessarily mean a horoscope with many squares and oppositions. Fundamentally it refers to the planetary positions in respect of the triplicities and quadruplicities. Thus, a watery planet in the fiery triplicity (such as the Moon in Aries) is harmonious; or an energetic planet in the mutable triplicity (such as Mars in Pisces). To go a step further, disharmony is shown by too many planets in their detriment or fall, or by too much mutual reception: such as Mars in a venusian sign aspecting Venus in a martial sign. Delineation must determine both the harmony and the disharmony of the horoscope; by working with the harmonious phases of the chart much of the disharmony may be overcome.

In the Orient the native's caste and rank are predetermined by heredity and tradition, but there is less restriction in the Occident. The log-cabin child may become president. Astrology emphasizes that all men are not equal. There is no reason, either esoterically or exoterically, why the mob should be more developed than the individual. On the contrary, astrology declares that the first necessity of spiritual growth is to develop independence and shake oneself free of the mob.

This is what is meant by saying that the native creates his own environment. This is the factor of independence found in the chart. The cardinal and mutable signs are generally more independent than the fixed. Air is higher than fire, and fire is higher than earth. Planets in their dignity have their greatest force, while those in their debility are stronger than those peregrine (without either dignity or debility). Thus the higher forces act more independently, and it should be determined whether the planetary positions in the chart bring out the higher or the lower forces. Aspects, while important, are still the last factors to be determined.

When this synthesis has been completed, attention may be directed to the fourth house and the determination reached there. The student astrologer will then realize the all-important truth that there is an intended fitness or unfitness between each individual and his environment: that birth as peer or peasant, in a university town or an industrial slum, whether the darling of the home or a neglected foundling, is all part of a definite plan.

The fourth house represents home, but not only the home that provides the childhood environment; it also indicates the home which the native creates for himself. Remember this is not a matter of simple analysis, but synthesizes where judgment must be used every step of the way. A favorable home may mean a luxurious mansion, a city apartment, or a gypsy wagon. For a gypsy the latter would be the most suitable, not the former. The definition of good depends on whether the native loves the open air, is a refined and leisurely patron of the arts, a businessperson, or a ne'er-do-well. Unfavorable influences in house four may indicate unending strain and worry, a filthy hovel, or a place where every note of luxury jars. A correct judgment must be based on the native's character, way of life, and other factors.

Astrological analysis has now been left far behind and the student is embarking upon the sea of true astrological interpretation. The chart is being read as a whole and not as a series of unrelated bits. The following suggestions will be of some assistance, but it is always necessary to study the individual horoscope first.

Planets in the Fourth House

Sun in the fourth means the native is attached to home. If unafflicted, he or she will make a good home, and hereditary influences are excellent.

Moon in the fourth gives the tendency to often change residence. If unafflicted, there are excellent hereditary influences from the mother. If afflicted by house eight or by the ruler of the eighth, the mother may die early in life or, in a feminine chart, there is danger of death in childbirth.

Mercury in the fourth says aspects are important, for good or ill. If ill, there can be much dissatisfaction in the home, many changes of residence, much roaming by the native. Note the planet aspecting most strongly.

Venus in the fourth house is very favorable for home life unless afflicted. The home atmosphere is refined. The native loves beautiful things there and much color.

Mars in the fourth house means the native is difficult at home, overcritical and argumentative. He may have trouble with his parents, or his home may be broken up through his own actions. Note the sign and aspects.

Jupiter in the fourth house gives a happy home life, especially during the latter half of life (unless seriously afflicted). The environment is conservative and well-to-do.

Saturn in the fourth house means that sign and aspects are important. If well-aspected, the native may own a home in the suburbs or country plus accumulate much property during life. If afflicted, life may end in poverty or reduced circumstances.

Uranus in the fourth house sometimes indicates a stepparent, at other times lack of harmony with parents, or sudden changes in domestic circumstances either for better or for worse.

Aspects are important. In its higher nature Uranus tends to give a fine home in the country, but if afflicted there is no home life at all so the native is a wanderer.

Neptune in the fourth house creates some secret or mystery in the home life, a skeleton in the closet. If close to the nadir, the circumstances of birth are peculiar. If afflicted, there is a clash with or through the parents. Because of the nature of Neptune, the aspects and sign position are important. In its higher nature Neptune gives good religious home surroundings; its lower nature produces deception, drinking, and carousing.

Pluto in the fourth house may mean the native was abandoned or orphaned as a child. Many natives were born near a war zone during raids or bombings. Drastic but often beneficial moves occur during childhood.

To make this lesson as helpful as possible, a further tabulation of the planets in the signs, when posited in the fourth house, is given. These thumbnail sketches, however, are only intended as suggestions and assume the planets to be favorably aspected. If afflicted, modifications must be made depending on the nature of the affliction. But they are only to be applied after determining all other factors of synthesis and adjusting the delineation to these factors.

These principles of delineation can be applied equally to any other house of the chart as interpreted in the light of that house's influence. Thus, for the first house, as related to personality; for the third, as related to brothers, sisters, neighbors, etc., etc., until all the houses have been considered.

Aries on the Fourth Cusp

Sun in Aries in the fourth house gives successful and fortunate parents and an excellent paternal heritage.

Moon in Aries in the fourth means the mother's influence is strong but not always fortunate.

Venus in Aries in the fourth means the native is strongly attached to his parents, but there are some differences.

Mars in Aries in the fourth gives sharp disputes and quarrels with parents plus danger of accidents to parents or early death of one, probably the father.

Jupiter in Aries in the fourth indicates that parents are religious, sympathetic, and helpful.

Saturn in Aries in the fourth gives unsatisfactory home life in childhood; the aspects are important.

Uranus in Aries in the fourth means the native is undisciplined, probably due to early loss of a parent, and although not the native's fault, punishment is often necessary.

Neptune in Aries in the fourth means a lack of understanding creates disharmony in the home.

Pluto in Aries in the fourth indicates power and control issues with the parents.

Taurus on the Fourth Cusp

Sun in Taurus in the fourth is fortunate for father. Stable home conditions and above-average wealth are in the home, which may be in the suburbs.

Moon in Taurus in fourth means the native is attached to mother and sisters, and their responsibilities may keep him at home until late in life.

Venus in Taurus in the fourth means family attachments are abnormally strong and the native may suffer from them. The native will spend much money to make the home attractive.

Mars in Taurus in the fourth means relatives create trouble in the home and should never live with the native.

Jupiter in Taurus in the fourth means relatives benefit from the native, who might provide a home for them.

Saturn in Taurus in the fourth can indicate early death of a brother as well as undue financial worries.

Uranus in Taurus in the fourth means rocky relationships with brothers, sisters, and neighbors.

Neptune in Taurus in the fourth brings misunderstandings in the home or with parents over financial matters.

Pluto in Taurus in the fourth indicates possible early death of a parent and potential for home-related natural disasters.

Gemini on the Fourth Cusp

Sun in Gemini in the fourth house gives a large family circle to which the native is devoted and many interests.

Moon in Gemini in the fourth gives many changes of residence. The native moves from city to city so there is a complete change from the childhood environment.

Venus in Gemini in the fourth means the marriage partner has many relatives.

Mars in Gemini in the fourth is scandal in family as well as arguments with brothers, sisters, and relatives.

Jupiter in Gemini in the fourth says the native is wealthier than other family members and spend money freely on home.

Saturn in Gemini in the fourth means native is ambitious but moody about home situations, and obtains help from relatives.

Uranus in Gemini in the fourth means the native has wanderlust and may leave home early in life. There are many changes of residence.

Neptune in Gemini in the fourth means the native likes to entertain but has little interest in home or relatives.

Pluto in Gemini in the fourth means much disruption and remodeling in the home.

Cancer on the Fourth Cusp

Sun in Cancer in the fourth house means the native has strong interest in home and probably has several children.

Moon in Cancer in the fourth means the native is very home-loving and domestic.

Venus in Cancer in the fourth means the native is passionately fond of home life and has a beautiful home.

Mars in Cancer in the fourth indicates clashes with a parent, probably early loss of father with the native having responsibility to care for the mother.

Jupiter in Cancer in the fourth means good home life with all family members in harmony.

Saturn in Cancer in the fourth means birth is difficult if near Nadir. The parents may be old and the native loses them early in life.

Uranus in Cancer in the fourth means the native is a roamer and uninterested in home life.

Neptune in Cancer in the fourth means, if near the Nadir, birth is difficult or there is some mystery surrounding parentage. The home is either highly religious or in some way strange and unfavorable.

Pluto in Cancer in the fourth means sharing resources, restoring of antique furniture, and several generations sharing the home.

Leo on the Fourth Cusp

Sun in Leo in the fourth house is fortunate for the native's father; heredity is good.

Moon in Leo in the fourth house means father or mother may have extramarital affairs, and thus the childhood home life is unsatisfactory; but native takes much pride in home.

Venus in Leo in the fourth means the father is musical and loves home.

Mars in Leo in the fourth gives ill-health or early loss of father.

Jupiter in Leo in the fourth means father is well-to-do and provides a good and harmonious home life.

Saturn in Leo in the fourth means father is advanced in years and denotes early senility.

Uranus in Leo in the fourth means a clash with father causes native to leave home early.

Neptune in Leo in the fourth means father is a heavy drinker or dope addict, causing much worry to native.

Pluto in Leo in the fourth means there is a false glamour in the home; father may have been killed before native's birth.

Virgo on the Fourth Cusp

Sun in Virgo in the fourth house means the native has relations in higher station in life; he is attached to brothers and sisters and is a good neighbor.

Moon in Virgo in the fourth means the native has indifferent relatives and spends money on health of mother.

Venus in Virgo in the fourth means relatives are very affectionate and native is much attached to children.

Mars in Virgo in the fourth means quarrels with relatives, frequently over friends of native.

Jupiter in Virgo in the fourth means relatives are well-to-do. Native is much attached to his or her own parents and to parents of spouse.

Saturn in Virgo in the fourth means early death of parent. Native is very practical about home matters and assumes much responsibility for home and relatives are poor but self-reliant.

Uranus in Virgo in the fourth means relatives are eccentric. Native changes residence frequently, probably to foreign country or to great distance from birthplace.

Neptune in Virgo in the fourth means the native has parasitic relatives and should avoid them; although closely attached to parents, misunderstandings arise.

Pluto in Virgo in the fourth means relatives are unique in their daily habits, perhaps even eccentric. Native may learn to be fanatic about caring for self.

Libra on the Fourth Cusp

Sun in Libra in the fourth house means good social position and native spends money freely on home.

Moon in Libra in the fourth means native is very domestic. Family is widely scattered but very attached.

Venus in Libra in the fourth means the native has beautiful home in which spouse takes great interest.

Mars in Libra in the fourth means strife with spouse plus loss of child or of parent early in life.

Jupiter in Libra in the fourth means wealthy marriage partner and peaceful home atmosphere.

Saturn in Libra in the fourth means much home responsibility and difficulty with marriage partner or very loyal marriage partner. Remainder of chart is extremely important.

Uranus in Libra in the fourth brings deaths, sudden upsets, and discord in the home.

Neptune in Libra in the fourth gives religious home life with much art and music; there is some mystery in home.

Pluto in Libra in the fourth house means being born into a new-age type family. Home may be anything from a tent to trailer, a castle to a camper.

Scorpio on the Fourth Cusp

Sun in Scorpio in the fourth house is legacy from father and much entertainment of friends in home.

Moon in Scorpio in the fourth is much sickness in home, probably of marriage partner. Hopes for legacy are not realized.

Venus in Scorpio in the fourth receives legacy from mother or from parents of spouse. Native is strongly attached to one parent and to home.

Mars in Scorpio in the fourth means much conniving for legacy and strife with spouse over money matters.

Jupiter in Scorpio in the fourth gives much extravagance, especially by spouse plus expenditures on health.

Saturn in Scorpio in the fourth means a very stern parent plus jealousy of relatives.

Uranus in Scorpio in the fourth means miscarriage or death of family member in infancy.

Neptune in Scorpio in the fourth means brothers and sisters are not to be trusted plus mysterious deaths in family.

Pluto in Scorpio in the fourth indicates that there are deep secrets within the family. Abusive relationships within the family are also possible.

Sagittarius on the Fourth House Cusp

Sun in Sagittarius in the fourth is good home life but with quarrels, probably over religion.

Moon in Sagittarius in the fourth means many changes of residence and native may live abroad. There is much similarity among members of family which may make for droll situations.

Venus in Sagittarius in the fourth gives a beautiful home with easygoing home life.

Mars in Sagittarius in the fourth means deaths in family

through accidents or fevers; differences with brothers, sisters, or neighbors; and an active family life generally.

Jupiter in Sagittarius in the fourth means a very generous spouse and a very religious home life with strong attachments.

Saturn in Sagittarius in the fourth gives a conservative home life; plus children may come late in life.

Uranus in Sagittarius in the fourth is a most unusual home life and the native is interested in technology.

Neptune in Sagittarius in the fourth means the family travels widely; the spouse is very spiritual, and the home life is marked by interest in the mystical.

Pluto in Sagittarius in the fourth indicates the family could live in another country or countries, and that the family is happy..

Capricorn on the Fourth House Cusp

Sun in Capricorn in the fourth house gives a deep interest in the home which is located in the suburbs or the country. The native entertains at home.

Moon in Capricorn in the fourth means the father is much older than the mother which brings family responsibilities to the native before marriage; children are not strong; and home is poorly managed.

Venus in Capricorn in the fourth is like the saying, "much ado about nothing," which makes the home life very unhappy.

Mars in Capricorn in the fourth brings early deaths *in* the family plus a jealous spouse.

Jupiter in Capricorn in the fourth is a generous and just home where the members of the family are very cooperative.

Saturn in Capricorn in the fourth means that an elderly parent lives with native after marriage. There are many family responsibilities and burdens which are well and successfully borne.

Uranus in Capricorn means the home is broken up early in life and the native suffers many disappointments.

Neptune in Capricorn in the fourth blends creativity with practicality. Creative work in the home is possible.

Pluto in Capricorn in the fourth indicates that the home will be extensively renovated at some point, or rebuilt because of severe damage.

Aquarius on the Fourth Cusp

Sun in Aquarius in the fourth means the family comes into the public eye, the vocation is carried on from the home, and a step-father is possible.

Moon in Aquarius in the fourth means family life is carried on in a place distant from place of birth, or the native establishes a new home at some distance. Home life is marked by unusual religious views and practices.

Venus in Aquarius in the fourth gives a beautiful home in which the native takes much pride and the spouse is an excellent social entertainer.

Mars in Aquarius in the fourth means that at some time the home is endangered by storms plus much illness and many accidents in the home.

Jupiter in Aquarius in the fourth means the family is involved in philanthropic or religious projects or communities.

Saturn in Aquarius in the fourth means the early death of father, brother, or older sister, as well as a home in the country.

Uranus in Aquarius in the fourth means the home is in a foreign land. It is a pioneering type of home, and you have an interest in antiques.

Neptune in Aquarius in the fourth means you may (or wish to) live near or on water. A parent could be absent or a substance abuser.

Pluto in Aquarius in the fourth indicates a strong-willed parent and an unusual home life.

Pisces on the Fourth House

Sun in Pisces in the fourth house gives a religious family which is much dependent on native and he should change residence to prevent undue reliance on him.

Moon in Pisces in the fourth means probable early death of mother. The native is a wanderer and has an unstable family life.

Venus in Pisces in the fourth means the native rises above the environment of birth and achieves a lovely home life, full of sympathy and understanding.

Mars in Pisces in the fourth gives immorality in home life; children may be begotten under unwholesome conditions, and there is much sickness in home.

Jupiter in Pisces in the fourth gives an excellent and bountiful home life; genius in family; plus deep interest in a home which .may be in a foreign country.

Saturn in Pisces in the fourth means parasitic relatives, early deaths in family, and little interest by native in a substantial home life.

Uranus in Pisces means fate (events beyond native's control) affects home life disastrously; caution is needed in all domestic affairs.

Neptune in Pisces in the fourth means your home can be a sanctuary, a peaceful place where you can meditate or re-center.

Pluto in Pisces in the fourth means your home could suffer water or severe weather damage.

Mercury has been omitted from all of the foregoing because, in respect of home life, it is neutral with some tendency for change. It represents the mental factor in home life and must be interpreted in light of its strongest aspect and sign position.

Remember, this list only offers suggestions to spark your thinking. No set of lessons, however complete, could fully cover problems of synthesis since, in the final analysis, every horoscope must be synthesized individually. By commencing with the principal indications of the chart and gradually working down to the details, lists such as the above will prove of real value.

Review Questions for Chapter 5

1. Is it possible for two children in the same family to have an entirely different relationship with each parent?

2. Does the home, as shown by the fourth house, have much effect during later life?

3. Rotate your own horoscope to locate in-laws, cousins, and great-grandparents in your own nativity. Are the descriptions like the people you know?

4. Can you analyze your brothers and sisters from your own horoscope?

5. What kind of home life do you need to be fulfilled?

|CHAPTER 6|

INDIVIDUAL RELATIONSHIPS

OBVIOUSLY A CORRECT INTERPRETATION OF THE native's relations with friends and enemies is of very great importance in any horoscope. It has already been noted that house eleven represents friends, house twelve represents secret enemies, and house seven represents open friends and enemies. But interpretation is more complicated. Synthesis, upon which the ultimate delineation must rest, demands a blending not only of the influences of houses and their rulers, but of the whole chart. The first phase of such delineation, in fact, is based upon the Ascendant and its ruler, the Sun, and the Moon. These signify the native's attitude toward friendship—whether he or she can make friends or is more prone to create enemies.

It is more true today than ever before that no man lives unto himself. The aborigine overcame the many obstacles in his life through physical strength and personal ability. Out of this developed the clan or family relationship which later expanded into the feudal state. Ultimately the social state emerged which is developed by the interaction among its members. The tendency today is to break down the national barriers of many social states and substitute for them a world state. Every person in our civilization is affected by these developments. Thus, the individual's relationship to other individuals has extended further and further until, today, his character and personality are of the utmost importance.

Friendship and enmity are the culmination of the individual's relationships with others and thus grow out of the native himself. They may be active or passive and may oscillate between these two states with changes in the native's environment. But certain basic qualities in the natal horoscope, which are themselves composites, will, when properly synthesized, indicate the native's responsibilities in these matters. If the horoscope shows the native to be self-centered, selfish, cruel, cold, or morose, one could hardly assign him a host of friends merely because his or her eleventh house is well aspected. On the other hand, if the native's house is weak, devoid of friends, and unaspected, it would be poor delineation to assert an absence of friends if the whole chart showed him to be hospitable, kind, affectionate, generous, and of fine character.

Horoscopic delineation is based upon reason, logic, and good sense. Rules are secondary and are to be used simply to direct the student's thinking into the correct channels. Thus, at the outset, define the native's character and determine his attitude toward friendship and enmity and then determine the attitude of others toward him to get the bases of the final judgment.

Planets as Friends

The Sun lends itself to dignified friendship. The native may be condescending, have friends in high places and positions of authority, plus have male friends (in a horoscope the Sun represents all males who have any contact with the native). The Sun lends permanence to friendships.

While the Moon signifies popularity, it also represents friendship with inferior persons or persons in a lower station. Generally, it represents all females who have any contact with the native. It makes friendships shallow and of short duration. The Moon represents the masses, the common people.

Mercury, as usual, depends upon its strongest aspect. In itself, however, it indicates superficiality, usually on the native's part, and is not strongly significant of friendship.

Venus is very desirable for friendships if on a high moral plane, being magnetic and attracting people (especially females) to the native. Venus friendships are usually affectionate, demonstrative, and emotional.

Mars more favors strong alliances than friendship in its usual sense, especially as regards persons of the native's own sex. The native is active and impulsive; his relations with those of the opposite sex are usually sexual (as is more apparent in horoscope comparison than from the native's chart alone).

Jupiter is an excellent planet for friendship. While not conducive to profound friendships, it brings a host of acquaintances and casual friends, much esteem from others, and a superficial jovial relationship to the world at large.

Saturn has been said to be unfavorable to friendship, but this is not true. Its friendships are neither superficial nor quickly made, but they are long-lasting, sincere, and trusting. The native's friends are either older, more mature, or more serious than himself, and sources of good advice and counsel.

Uranus brings sudden friendships that are often short. They may be unusual, fantastic, or based upon common interests. Friends may be eccentric or the native's attitude toward others may be eccentric.

Friends brought by a strong well-placed Neptune sometimes give the native deep spiritual insight. The friendship may be aesthetic or platonic but, due to man's general inability to attune himself to Neptune, it often brings distress and trouble to the native. The friend may be deceitful or have ulterior motives, and the native's character and ability to withstand temptation is probably more important when Neptune dominates the sphere of friendship than at any other time.

Pluto indicates the acquaintance or group contact rather than the personal friend. Sometimes these are coworkers in reform movements, other persons interested in occult phenomena, or technicians sharing a common social or psychological premise. Pluto also represents mobs or large gatherings of people.

Planets as Foes

The same general principles apply to the question of the planets and enmity.

The Sun brings hostility from persons in high positions as well as troubles from superiors in profession or employment.

The Moon indicates false friends, enmity from persons of low station, and hostility due to jealousy and avarice.

Mercury (again depending on aspect) indicates the slanderous type of enemy, the backbiter, persons who talk badly about the native or libel him in writing.

Venus is difficult to reconcile with enmity and it more often indicates friendships that harm or debase the native. Since Venus is a feminine planet, it is more dangerous in a masculine horoscope. Afflictions to Venus are also important.

Mars brings violent enemies, persons who will do the native physical harm. It operates in the female horoscope in much the same way as Venus in a male chart. Licentiousness in friendship may bring harm to the native.

Jupiter brings enmity from bigoted persons or through causes associated with bigotry; enmities caused by Jupiter often find expression in lawsuits. Usually these are open enemies.

Saturn brings secret enemies and enmities of long duration, ambitious enemies who will hold a grudge and bide their time to wreak vengeance.

Uranus brings sudden enmities for unknown reasons, eccentric enemies, and enemies who strike back quickly but do not hold to their enmity.

Neptune brings the most treacherous type of enemies, persons who will not stop at anything to attain their ends. The cause of the enmity may be mysterious, or it may be based upon some fancied wrong.

Pluto brings sly and subtle enemies who are ruthless in their aims, friends who attempt to coerce the native to act at their direction, and fanatics. There can be psychological torture as well as physical abuse in extreme cases.

Because all planets are in every chart and each life is different from every other, the influence of any planet on friendship and enmity is determined only through careful synthesis of the chart. The general indications noted above must be weighed against sign and house positions and the configurations to each planet, all of this being related to the native's character and environment.

Signs as Friends or Foes

Authors have written much on the influence of the signs for friendship and enmity. Actually, all signs are friendly, and any sign can be antagonistic. Through their quadruplicities they indicate the quality, and through their triplicities the plane of action of any planet found in them or of the houses in which they are placed. However, some signs are more prone than others to be friendly, unfriendly, or solitary.

Aries is often called a solitary sign because of its aggressive independence.

Taurus is sometimes considered a solitary sign because of its false pride, obstinacy, and fixity of opinion.

Gemini, the strongest sign for popularity, is often considered unfriendly because of the native's tendency to ride roughshod over others and his general thoughtlessness and disregard for the rights of others.

Cancer is considered friendly because of its receptivity and consideration for others. Its emotional nature and maternal associations also have much to do with friendliness. But, like all water signs, it is secretive.

Leo is actively good for friendship, particularly that type of friendship where the native acts as advisor.

Virgo is often considered a solitary sign because of its timidity.

Libra is probably the friendliest sign in a passive sense. It is basically a sign of companionship and understanding of the other.

Scorpio is probably the least friendly sign except where the emotions or passions are involved. It is heedless of the rights of others and sometimes distinctly fond of hostility.

Sagittarius is decidedly the most active and friendly sign. It is jovial, generous, and hail-fellow-well-met.

Capricorn is deeply sincere in friendship but is usually regarded as unfriendly because of its egoism and coldly calculating determination to achieve its ambitions.

Aquarius is often considered solitary because of its eccentricity and failure to meet others on common ground. In its highest element, however, Aquarius is an understanding sign appreciating the rights of others.

Pisces, while truly a passively friendly sign, is often regarded as unfriendly because it can be parasitical, treacherous, and false. It can also be mean and tyrannical but, in the author's experience, it more often indicates puppy-like devotion to friends. It is not aggressive and friendship must be brought to it.

The foregoing should be taken only as suggestive in preparing the horoscope. As an example of how this information might be synthesized, assume an individual whose chart indicates a well-balanced and generous character who is jovial and full of fun, with Sagittarius rising. There is a house interception so that Scorpio is in house eleven and Mars in Pisces is in house four. This suggests friends taking advantage of the native's friendliness, leading to treachery and misunderstanding. If Jupiter is trine Mars, the native is able to cope with such friends, but if Saturn is square Mars, the native's home life is adversely affected by the jealous avarice of these friends. By weighing all these factors when selecting his friends the native can avoid these situations.

Favorable aspects between planets indicate friendliness on the part of persons indicated by house rulership, sign, and position. Afflictions tend to indicate enemies (true for both sign and house rulership). Thus, a native with a seriously afflicted Jupiter in Scorpio should not select friends from among persons with Scorpio, Sagittarius, or Pisces strong in their charts or with the Sun in these signs.

Houses As Friends Or Foes

While the Ascendant indicates the native's attitude toward friendship and the Descendant the attitude of others toward him, house XI is known as the house of friendship as well as the house of hopes and wishes so planets in this house often indicate the type of friends to be expected in the native's social life. When benefic planets are placed therein, or if the ruler is well-placed and aspected, true friendship can be expected. But friendship is not limited to house eleven or to social life. Occupational or professional friends fall under the tenth house, friendships in the environment of employment under house six, religious friendships under house nine, etc. Business associates are indicated by houses seven, 10, or six.

In all questions of friendship in the general sense, the eleventh house is to be considered together with the sign on its cusp, the planets in it, and the position and configurations of its ruler. But house five is equally important for friendship with persons of the opposite sex, which can be friendship leading to love. When the nature of the friendship is in doubt, houses five and eight (sex) are to be considered and, indeed, this same principle should be followed with respect to friendships in any house.

Thus, friendships related to the second house often have to do with economic matters; friendships made on journeys will be associated with the third or ninth house; friendships with neighbors, or friends acquired through brothers and sisters, will be associated with the third house; those relating to home life or to a parent (or to entertainment of friends in the home) are associated with the fourth house; house six will indicate friendships with fellow employees, in the employment environment, or with persons (such as servants) in a lower station; house seven can indicate friendships through marriage or partnerships (friendships) entered into for mutual profit; in their higher vibrations, friendships associated with house eight can indicate a common interest in the occult but more often have a sexual component, particularly when with the opposite sex; the friendships indicated by house nine may arise through mutual interest in church, philosophical, or occult matters, but these configurations more frequently relate to platonic friendships or friendships of an idealistic nature; tenth house friendships are through a parent, through employment, or with employers; house twelve friendships are always secretive in nature and can prove detrimental to the native.

If the ruler of house twelve is found in house eleven and well configured, the native has the ability to convert enemies into friends by using diplomacy. Likewise, when the cusps of the tenth and eleventh houses are covered by the same sign, the native can make friends of his superiors in employment; this also indicates friendships with honorable people. But when the same sign covers the cusps of houses eleven and twelve, the native risks converting friends into enemies by his own actions.

Secret Enemies

In addition to being the house of partnerships, house seven is also the house of open enemies. This is readily understood when it is remembered that enemies are always indicated by afflictions, and friends by favorable configurations. But house twelve is the house of secret enemies or treacherous friends. House seven is associated with Libra and Venus, while twelve is associated with Pisces, Neptune, and Jupiter.

In synthesizing house twelve factors as they relate to enemies, the investigation must go further than the sign ruling this house, the planets in it, and the sign and house position of its ruler. Once the native's character has been synthesized, the following general factors of house rulership are to be considered

Rulers in the Twelfth House

The ruler of the Ascendant in house 12 indicates secret enemies produced by the native's own actions; likewise, the same sign on the twelfth and first house cusps indicates that the native is his or her own worst enemy. The ruler of twelfth in the first also causes the native to bring about his or her own undoing. When the ruler of the Ascendant is in the twelfth, the native is handicapped by an inferiority complex.

The ruler of the second house in the twelfth is a warning to the native against being cheated in business or finance and, if this is a malefic planet, can bring financial ruin. The ruler of twelfth in the second can lead the native to bring about his or her own undoing by cheating in such matters.

The ruler of house third house in the twelfth indicates enmities through neighbors or family members; if afflicted, the native may do injury to members of his family. It also warns the native to guard his or her correspondence to avoid making enemies in this way. The ruler of the twelfth house in the third says be careful not to make enemies on journeys or enemies may write slanderous stories about the native.

The ruler of house the fourth house in the twelfth indicates enemies in the native's own home; if a malefic, enemies may cause much difficulty and unhappiness when the native is past middle age. The ruler of the twelfth house in the fourth may cause the native to connive against members of his or her own household; a parent is also repressive.

The ruler of the fifth house in house 12 brings secret love affairs which can make enemies; note carefully the planets involved. The ruler of the twelfth in the fifth brings broken love interests through the native's actions, sometimes turning a sweetheart into an enemy. It also causes estrangement of parent from child.

The ruler of house six in the twelfth indicates hostile relations with work associates or in the employment environment. It also indicates hospitalization under unfavorable conditions and, if malefic, will indicate unfriendly treatment, rude and inattentive medical personnel, etc. The ruler of the twelfth house in the sixth works in much the same manner, but here it is more due to the native's own actions.

The ruler of the seventh house in the twelfth indicates open enemies who are also treacherous; their antagonism can be overcome only through strong efforts on the native's part. It sometimes indicates an elopement. The ruler of the twelfth house in the seventh is a warning that enemies may arise through partnerships, marriage, or business.

The ruler of the eighth house in the twelfth means the native is his or her own enemy through sexual relationships that can impair his or her health; it also indicates a deliberate attempt to deprive the native of an inheritance. If the planet is malefic, violence may be indicated. The ruler of twelfth in the eighth means the native may connive to obtain an inheritance, thus creating enemies.

The ruler of the ninth house in the twelfth house indicates hypocritical enemies, especially if Mercury is involved in any way. It also indicates enemies at law. The ruler of the twelfth house in the ninth warns of loss through lawsuits when malefic; if benefic, the native may win lawsuits through intrigue. Both positions also indicate bigoted enemies.

The ruler of the tenth house in the twelfth house indicates enemies in the native's profession who could undermine his or her position. In a feminine chart this indicates enemies in social life. The ruler of the twelfth house in the tenth says the native's ambition to succeed may create enemies.

The ruler of the eleventh house in the twelfth house indicates the unhappy faculty of turning friends into enemies; or, alternately, well-meaning friends who do harm. The ruler of the twelfth house in the eleventh means the native turns enemies into friends or might undermine friends in order to advance himself or herself.

The ruler of the twelfth house in the twelfth house helps neutralize any otherwise malefic influences exerted by this house. The same is true if the ruler of the twelfth house is exalted by sign in another house.

Quadruplicities as Friends or Foes

Quadruplicities must not be overlooked in this delineation as they often furnish clues of great value. A cardinal sign on the house eleven cusp indicates active friendships and ambitious friends; on the twelfth cusp it indicates aggressive enemies who are clever in finding ways to injure the native.

A fixed sign on the eleventh house cusp indicates deep friendships with persons who are loyal and faithful; on the twelfth house cusp they indicate tenacious enemies who retain their antagonism.

A mutable sign on the eleventh house cusp indicates superficial friendships with fickle and inconsequential persons; on the twelfth house cusp, it gives enemies whose bark is worse than their bite and who soon lose their hostility.

Horoscope Comparison

While this is a large field that cannot be encompassed in a single lesson, certain fundamentals may be of much value to the student.

An astrologer is frequently asked if a new acquaintance is likely to prove to be friend or enemy. This can be ascertained in many ways, one of which is to calculate a chart for the moment of meeting or for the moment the question was asked. While an answer requires knowledge of progressions and transits, in fact the whole field of horary astrology (not covered by this course), the present ephemeral positions of the celestial bodies will suggest which planet in the natal chart is the significator. When that planet has been ascertained, the chart should be turned in such a way as to place that planet on the Ascendant. If the aspects and transiting aspects are then noted and interpreted in the light of the information given thus far in the present lesson, very accurate determinations can be achieved.

In such cases, however, it is better to obtain the birth data of the new acquaintance and then compare the two charts. Such questions usually arise in connection with possible marriage or a business deal or partnership. Although the principles are the same, they must be interpreted in function of the probable relationship.

Thus, in respect of marriage, it is best if the Venus in each chart is in favorable aspect to the Sun of the other chart. If the Mars of one chart favorably aspects to the Sun of the other chart, there is strong physical (largely sexual) attraction. Saturn in one chart conjunction or favorable to the Sun or Ascendant in the other causes the native with Saturn to become dependent on the other. Of course, favorable aspects of the benefic Jupiter to any planet in the other chart will indicate benefits along the lines suggested by that planet's position.

One of the most ancient rules is that the Sun of the woman's horoscope conjunction or in good aspect to the Moon of the man's chart favors marriage. In the author's experience, however, this configuration does not necessarily mean a magnetic attraction. While it indicates harmony, marriages (unless purely platonic) must be based on more than just harmony. A perfect marriage requires psychological (mental), spiritual, and physical (sexual) harmony.

In all cases the luminaries must be considered, especially in their relationship to other planets. While some astrologers hold that malefics in one horoscope falling upon luminaries in the other (even when favorable) indicate enmity and difficulties and that benefics (even when unfavorably aspected) indicate harmony, this has not been the author's experience. As already mentioned, Saturn can tie two people very closely so the whole question is whether the luminaries are well-aspected. Mars in a male chart aspecting the Sun in a female chart indicates strong sexual attraction; if this is a favorable aspect and the Sun in the female horoscope is unafflicted, this tie is wholly favorable even though Mars is a malefic planet.

The principles of interpreting a natal chart may be applied generally to the comparison of horoscopes, with one principal exception: opposition aspects between two charts, especially when of the opposite sex, are not to be regarded as malefic. They follow the principle of the blending of opposites, i.e., the complementary nature of opposite signs (see Table 9).

Table 9. Zodiac Signs and Opposites

Aries	Libra
Taurus	Scorpio
Gemini	Sagittarius
Cancer	Capricorn
Leo	Aquarius
Virgo	Pisces

Mars in a female chart opposing Venus in a male chart indicates sexual attraction. If these planets are otherwise favorably located, this is harmonious; if otherwise unfavorable, this can be unfavorable.

There are too many possible interrelations between two horoscopes to be included here. However, one general principle can be given which is *to strike a balance by evaluating the attractions and repulsions at work between the two charts.* List them, allowing a point for each. Then list the favorable aspects, allowing a point for each. Finally, list the favorable and house sign positions, also allowing one point for each. Each planet can thus obtain a maximum of four points.

The same procedure is then followed for unfavorable aspects, sign and house positions, as well as for attraction and repulsion. If the result of summing these points is almost even, the two parties will be indifferent to one another, however if the favorable positions far outbalance the unfavorable ones there is a strong chance of a successful marriage. Of course, this is only a statistical approach, and the strength or debility of the planets in each chart is also important.

The following is also valuable in regard to attraction and repulsion:

Mercury causes attraction or repulsion on intellectual grounds (leaving aside the strongest aspect to Mercury).

Venus, a strongly magnetic planet, causes attraction or repulsion on grounds of emotion, affection, and feeling.

Mars attracts or repels for carnal, physical, or sexual attraction.

Jupiter attracts or repels for reasons of form, decorum, and adherence to custom.

Saturn attracts or repels on grounds of ambition or critical judgment.

Uranus attracts or repels (depending much on the aspects) for reasons of originality or unconventionality.

Neptune attracts or repels for obscure reasons, probably related to spiritual or aesthetic matters.

Pluto attracts or repels for unexplained reasons related to strong sexual pulls as well as mystical or psychological reasons.

The house or mundane positions of the planets, although of less importance, must also be considered. This is applicable with respect to luminary or angular position, particularly if the Sun is in the Ascendant in one chart and the Moon in the Ascendant in the other, as this means harmony between them from the mundane viewpoint. The Sun would stabilize the changeable Moon, and the Moon would lend variety to the fixed Sun. Likewise, the Sun in a male chart falling on the Midheaven in a female chart indicates that the woman would look up to the man while benefitting in some public way from association with him. The Moon in the female chart operates similarly for the male.

Other mundane examples are planets in the seventh house of one horoscope falling upon the eleventh house of the other which may be beneficial; similarly, planets in house seven of one horoscope falling in the twelfth house of the other may be harmful.

These same principles can be applied to progressed charts. The date, time, and place of meeting are important. These dates and others are more easily determined by considering the applicable aspects in the progressed horoscopes and their directions as well as by comparing them, than from one map alone. But too much stress should not be placed on the progressed chart in comparison work, since favorable progressed aspects too often bring attachments which pass as the planets progress away from the particular aspect.

An easy way to look at planetary relations between two horoscopes is to place the celestial bodies into a biwheel chart in two concentric rings, as shown in Figures 4, 5, and 6.

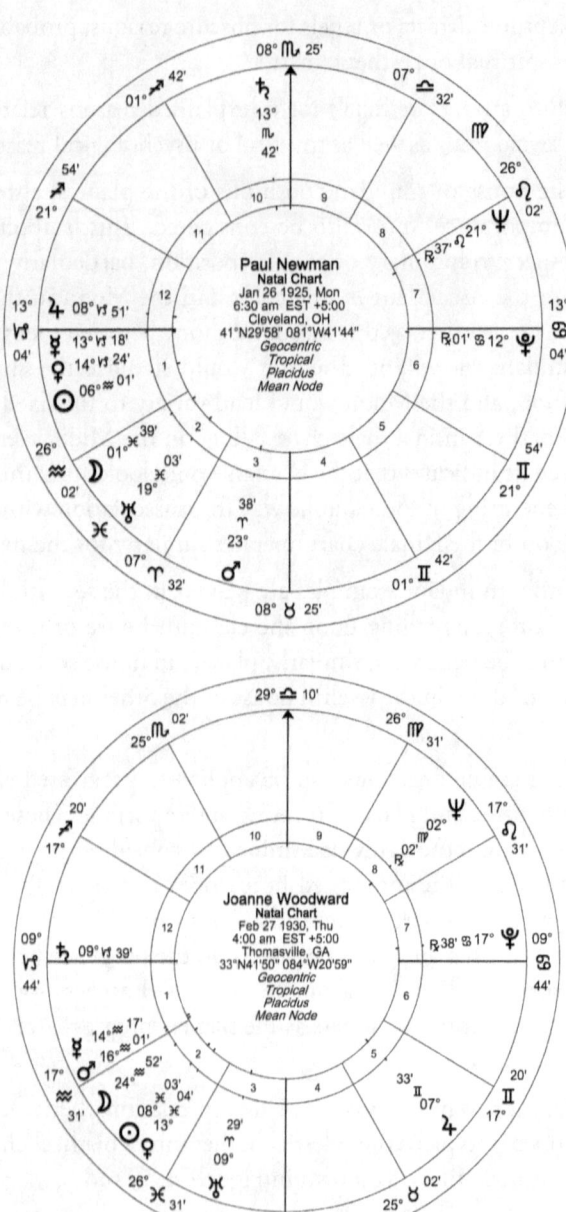

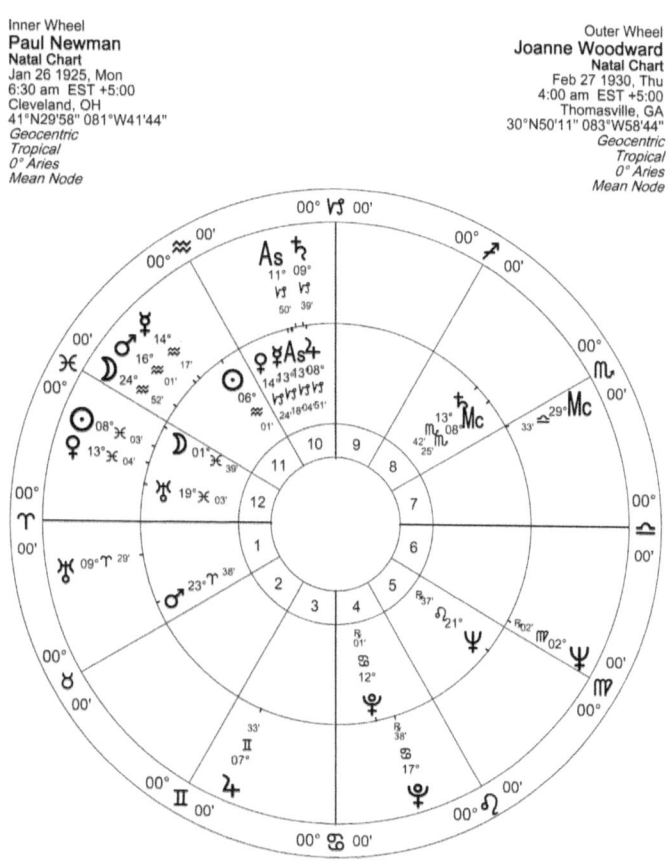

Review Questions for Chapter 6

1. Is the most recent acquaintance you made going to be a friend or foe according to your chart?

2. Must you be on guard against secret enemies?

3. Prepare a horoscope comparison between yourself and your best friend.

|Chapter 7|

Love Relationships

Probably more has been written about love and the fifth house than on all the rest of astrology put together, although much of this seems based more on fantasy than on fact. In any case, the student must devote very close attention to the love factors in a horoscope as well as to the marriage factors.

The difference between love and marriage must be recognized at the outset; there may be real love without marriage as well as real marriage without love, although the difference between them may not be well marked in the horoscope. A horoscope too strong in its emotional or love factors might not be a good marrying chart, while an intensely domestic and marrying horoscope might be entirely lacking in the more fiery love elements. Domesticity, affection, and responsiveness do not necessarily mean love as it is understood in today's world.

Poets have described love as a condition of the heart, whereas it is more probably one of the pituitary gland which is, in turn, connected with emotions. But true love is a compound of spiritual kinship, mental harmony, and physical desire. Rarely are these three essentials in proper balance, or even properly understood, at the time of marriage. While love at first sight does occur at times, what is seen to be love (whether at first sight or even at the time of marriage) is simply physical attraction, the lowest of the three elements. True love must grow and be constantly readjusted, nurtured in the combined experiences of the man and the woman; it is a principle of nature related to the evolution of the individual and his growth in intellectual and spiritual understanding. Indeed, the growth of love into a permanent relationship depends almost entirely on the understanding the individual brings to it plus his ability to readjust constantly to changing circumstances. In this connection the astrologer has a definite advantage over all others in possessing foreknowledge of future influences and thus being able to prepare for them.

The safe course is to commence the synthesis of the emotional elements in a chart with the lowest factor, physical desire, since it is indeed rare to find mental harmony and spiritual kinship without physical desire, especially if the individuals concerned are younger than 40 or 45. There do exist exceptional instances of marriages which are truly made in heaven and remain there, but these are rare; a man and a woman will also at times enter into marriage on the basis of mental harmony alone, but this is even more rare. In the vast majority of cases the first basis of love is physical desire.

Before synthesizing the love factors in a horoscope the native's character and personality must be determined. The native with good character and balanced personality, who can exercise self-control, will react much more adequately to inharmonious love factors than the one whose emotions run rampant. Similarly, as mentioned in the chapter on individual relationships the friendly person will react more favorably to love than the highly individualistic, self-centered, egotistic, or inhibited one. When all of these questions have been answered, look first to house five, then to house eleven, and finally to houses three and nine. In this way love is approached first through its physical side (fifth, not eighth, which is strictly speaking the house of sensuous desire), then through the refining element of friendship (eleventh), next mental harmony (third), and spiritual kinship (ninth), thus completing the cycle.

Similarly (leaving aside questions of house rulership) Venus, the planet of love, must be considered first in relation to these houses as affected by the native's character and then in relation to these houses as affected by the native's character and then in relation to each of the celestial bodies in the chart: Mars for passion, Jupiter for form, Saturn for restraint, Uranus for orthodoxy and romanticism, Neptune for idealism, Pluto for desire, and the Sun and Moon for confirmatory influences including romanticism.

Hence the need to grasp the chart as a whole, as in all synthesis, to understand it as a single unit reflecting the native's whole life, studying carefully the strength, influence, and avenues of expression (houses) of Venus as related to each of the four houses playing a major role with respect to love.

Next after Venus in importance are the influences of Mars and the Moon on the native's love life: Mars for its physical energy and the Moon for the element of romance. If Mars dominates the chart or these three houses, the native's passion is stressed, while the Moon would excite the imagination. In another sense, also, the Moon is very important for interpreting the masculine horoscope, for it represents generally all the women who might influence a man's life. The Sun has the same function in the feminine chart.

Thus it must be determined at the outset which of the houses affecting love life predominate and what strengths they possess as indicated by sign rulership, the positions of the rulers, and the planets found in them. This permits a determination of the emotional strength of Venus, Mars, and the Moon for synthesis of these factors yields a fundamental picture of the native's love life as well as of the person to whom he will respond.

The quadruplicity and triplicity influences must be borne in mind as well, for a water-Moon-house five combination will differ entirely from a water-Venus-house eleven combination or any different combination dominating houses three or nine.

Likewise, a water-Moon-house three combination dominating the other three houses will behave differently from the same combination on either of the other three houses. The most difficult combinations, perhaps, are those which clash internally, as, for example, a water-Mars-house nine one.

The importance of Venus has been overemphasized. While this planet is important, it is not the sole criterion of the love factors in a horoscope. Human nature is far too subtle and complicated for that. Venus is receptive like the magnet which attracts love. Alone it does not initiate love but draws this ecstatic state to the native. Mars is the planet which gives love and, when it dominates the love factors in a horoscope, the native is aggressive in love, sometimes expending all his energy on the object of his affections plus demanding the same in return.

While astrology is governed by certain rules, a horoscope is ultimately a portrait of the native's personality, individuality, and character—not a mere tabulation of indications.

It reveals the owner's humanity and as such portrays a living, throbbing, physical, mental, and emotional creature—a synthesis of the elements which make up a living being.

The aspects are important, since love is the deepest emotion man can experience. The emotional side of life is the most difficult to control. Reason is controlled by logic, but emotions arise from personal desires; thus, while logic can help overcome inharmonious aspects as they relate to the mental life, the control of desire is much more difficult. For this reason the aspects are very important.

Planets As Love Factors

The relationship of the celestial bodies to the love factors in a horoscope may be summarized as follows. While they are presented more or less according to their general astrological importance for love factors, this order of importance may differ from that shown in the particular horoscope.

Venus is the planet of refinement, expecting that in love and returning what it has received. It is the planet of love and also the planet of pleasure; hence, when afflicted, the pleasure it offers may be indolent sensuality. Venus is also the planet of longing for mysticism, especially when under Pisces influence. Venus is quietly demonstrative, but more so in the air signs.

Mars is the planet of energy and vitality and thus overemphasizes the passionate and carnal side of the love relationship. It is dynamic and aggressive and lends impulsiveness to love; as well as refusing to take "No" for an answer. The native with a well-placed and well-aspected Mars (probably because of its primitive nature) will be unfailingly protective toward the object of love but also unfailingly loyal. Mars is particularly demonstrative in the earth signs. With this planet the triplicities are especially important.

Moon lends imagination, romance, and sometimes fickleness to the love nature. It is receptive; it can give intensity to the love experience or can cause inconstant curiosity, depending upon the aspects. The Moon is non-aggressive. Aspects between the Moon and Venus or Mars are exceedingly important, as are the sign and house positions. The Moon will often give a maternal tinge to the love nature, and, in a masculine chart, the Moon in a fixed sign lends permanence to the affections.

Sun lends restraint to the love life and has a strong tendency to dominate the object of affection. While there is a strong desire to give, this may be coupled with vanity and egoism, particularly under affliction. In a feminine chart the Sun in a fixed sign lends permanence to the affections. Its sign and house are always important.

Mercury reflects the body which aspects it most strongly so it is difficult to assign an all-inclusive principle to this planet. Mercury may be .associated with the intellectual dimension of love and may also give a dual love interest. Apart from all other factors, it must be determined if Mercury is most strongly influenced by Venus, the Moon, or Mars. Note carefully Mercury's strength by aspect, sign, and house position, as its influence may range from one extreme to the other, i.e., from fidelity to superficiality and from ingrowing sensuality to impotence. Thus, Mercury is very important for the love factors in a chart.

Jupiter, when well positioned and strongly influencing the love factors, causes the native to abide by tradition, form, and the social conventions, even leading this individual to subordinate his emotions to what is deemed fitting and proper. While preventing loose conduct, this may also inhibit a normal and healthy expression of the native's love nature. Jupiter sometimes brings celibacy. Its house position is very important.

Saturn gives ambition in love, but it is restrictive, restraining, cold, or disappointing, usually because of the native's basic character. Especially when afflicted, it places almost insurmountable obstacles in the path of a normal love life. But when in favorable relationship to Venus, Saturn makes the native loyal. It may also cause him to be cold, calculating and, when afflicting Venus (especially in a feminine horoscope), may make the love life vulgar. The signs and aspects are most important, with the houses less so.

Uranus acts in a dual manner. It is sudden, bringing love at first sight and elopement, most often when in house twelve or when that house is implicated. When afflicted, it brings sudden love affairs which are terminated just as suddenly. Uranus makes the love life original; this may be expressed in an unorthodox manner or through unorthodox attachments, either for good or bad, depending on the native's character and other factors in the chart. The strength of Uranus's influence on the native's character is important.

Neptune makes the love life run to extremes, being drastically good or drastically bad, most often the latter. It brings into the love nature the elements of mimicry, masquerade, and fantasy. While a highly spiritual planet, it is just as strongly a sexual planet. Mars stimulates the passions and Jupiter highlights the formal side of the love life, but Neptune either leads to celibacy (complete denial of a sex life) or brings perversion, particularly if house eight is involved. If the ninth house is involved, it may make the love life mystical. Aspects are of the greatest importance, with the houses next in importance and the signs last.

Pluto makes the love life either very sensual or brings in a touch of brutality. The partners may seek to either change each other or drift into a pattern of supporter and leaner. There is always an intensity of emotional reactions.

House five is primarily concerned with the personal side of love, house eleven with the associational side of the love life (consider also its ruler), and house nine with the spiritual side (consider its ruler as well).

If the ruler of the fifth house is found in the first, there is a tendency toward love of self; in house two, love of money; in house three, love of sibling; in house four, love of home and parent; in house six, a tendency to an inferior station in life, as an employee or associated with an employee; in house eight it helps center the affections on the marriage partner; in house eight, the love nature is excessively centered on sex, but if well aspected there may be a love of the occult or some interest in the occult; in house nine, idealism in love (celibacy if Neptune or Jupiter rule house five and are in house nine, love of pleasure and association; or in house twelve, secret love affairs usually with a married person, widow, or widower.

It would be quite impossible to give all the rules that have been proposed to cover the love factors in horoscopes. In any case, they arise from the astrological fundamentals with which the student is by now familiar. For example, an afflicted Mars in the Ascendant, and in the venusian signs, would indicate lack of modesty in a feminine horoscope; while in a masculine horoscope an afflicted Venus in the Ascendant, and in the martian signs, would be a sure indication of sensuality.

Signs as Love Factors

As a suggestive guide for the student the following list has been prepared of planetary positions in each of the 12 signs when posited in house five. Knowledge of the quality of action conferred on each celestial body by each sign will make it possible to expand this foundation and construct similar lists for the other houses as they relate to house five. But it must be borne in mind that this list is strictly suggestive, giving fundamental factors which will invariably undergo considerable modification in each individual horoscope. The list is designed primarily to reveal the favorable side of each influence, but the aspects may alter this and cause the native to exemplify the lower or unfavorable side.

Hence the following is information on the fundamental nature of each sign on the cusp of house five without modification by the sign in which the ruler of house five is found or by the nature of any aspects to it:

Aries on the Fifth Cusp

Aries on the fifth house cusp is ardent, impetuous, and impulsive in love, aggressive, and in danger of making mistakes.

Sun in Aries, ruler of the fifth, gives an ambitious and courageous lover but danger of overreaching in love.

Moon in Aries, ruler of the fifth, is fanciful, romantic, egotistic, and headstrong in love, but brings danger of inconstancy.

Mercury in Aries, ruler of the fifth, is mentally aggressive toward the opposite sex and thinks a great deal about romance (note aspects carefully).

Venus in Aries, ruler of the fifth, is demonstrative and oversexed, but inclined to be idealistic.

Mars in Aries, ruler of the fifth, is reckless and ardent in love, stronger in a feminine chart than in a masculine one.

Jupiter in Aries, ruler of the fifth, is ambitious in love and tends to be reckless, but this is due more to changeability (note aspects).

Saturn in Aries, ruler of the fifth, gives difficulties in love affairs and is jealous and revengeful.

Uranus in Aries, ruler of the fifth, is impetuous, unorthodox, jealous, and loose.

Neptune in Aries, ruler of the fifth, gives a dog-like devotion, eroticism, and a tendency to form attachments with inferior persons; this is not a good position and the aspects should be carefully noted.

Pluto in Aries is ardent in love, pursuing love connections with much intensity.

Taurus on the Fifth Cusp

Taurus on the fifth house cusp tends to sensuality.

Sun in Taurus, ruler of the fifth, is proud in love, and has a strong attachment to youthful persons and children (including the native's own children).

Moon in Taurus, ruler of the fifth, brings intrigue into the love life; the native is affectionate and vivacious.

Mercury in Taurus, ruler of the fifth, gives an interest in erotic literature; love of reading about love (note aspects); and when unaspected, rather barren of love but fondness of discussing it.

Venus in Taurus, ruler of the fifth who displays personal charm and is attracted to dynamic and charming persons.

Mars in Taurus, ruler of the fifth, is not always reliable, but is passionate and precocious in love.

Jupiter in Taurus, ruler of the fifth, is very modest toward the opposite sex and in love affairs; decorum and social requirements play an important part (note aspects).

Saturn in Taurus, ruler of the fifth, is, until middle life, more interested in money and creates an attachment to an older person, probably because of his or her wealth.

Uranus in Taurus, ruler of the fifth, has odd love affairs ranging from the romantic to the platonic (aspects and position of Venus are important).

Neptune in Taurus, ruler of the fifth, is the languorous type and very sexy.

Pluto in Taurus is sensual and passionate, a charmer.

Gemini on the Fifth Cusp

Gemini on the fifth cusp gives dual love affairs, an irregular love life, and indifference to the moral proprieties.

Sun in Gemini, ruler of the fifth, is rather vain about love affairs, egotistic in love and in a feminine chart shows the likelihood of two or more lovers at once.

Moon in Gemini, ruler of the fifth, is fickle in love, idle about romance, forever chasing rainbows, and, in a masculine chart, shows more than one sweetheart at a time.

Mercury in Gemini, ruler of the fifth, thinks about love a great deal and inclines to be flighty in love affairs (again aspects are important).

Venus in Gemini, ruler of the fifth, is very demonstrative and fickle in love, and has more love of a good time than love of a lover (aspects are important).

Mars in Gemini, ruler of the fifth, is changeable in love, dynamic, active in love affairs, and has more than one affair at a time.

Jupiter in Gemini, ruler of the fifth, has love affairs that go to extremes, either very decorous or scandalous (aspects are important).

Saturn in Gemini, ruler of the fifth, forms attachments to

a much older person, secret love affairs, and is calculating and cold in love affairs.

Uranus in Gemini, ruler of the fifth, has many love affairs of very short duration fickleness, dual love affairs, and sudden attachments which may be transferred almost at will, since they are almost more in the head than in the heart.

Neptune in Gemini, ruler of the fifth, is reckless and chaotic in love affairs and may meet a sweetheart through travel.

Pluto in Gemini, ruler of the fifth, loves a neighbor, is extremely sensual, and tends to thwart open communication between lovers.

Cancer on the Fifth Cusp

Cancer on the fifth cusp brings sentimental love affairs in which there is danger of inconstancy, strong maternal instincts, and faithfulness if the emotions are truly involved.

Sun in Cancer, ruler of the fifth, has very emotional love affairs plus usually some interference in love life, often from the mother.

Moon in Cancer, ruler of the fifth, gives emotional instability and very sentimental love affairs (aspects are important, as affairs may bring sorrow).

Mercury in Cancer, ruler of the fifth, gives a native who is sensitive about love affairs which are usually very superficial.

Venus in Cancer, ruler of the fifth, is eager for attention and loves display and desires to be worshiped in love.

Mars in Cancer, ruler of the fifth, is strongly attractive to opposite sex; in feminine chart, this brings popularity with the opposite sex but danger of excessive emotionalism.

Jupiter in Cancer, ruler of the fifth, gives great popularity and is very decorous in love but romantic.

Saturn in Cancer, ruler of the fifth, brings sorrow through

love affairs; the native is strongly affected by love affairs which, although worthwhile, lead to sorrow.

Uranus in Cancer, ruler of the fifth, enjoys originality in love; the native has emotional and fantastic ideas about love.

Neptune in Cancer, ruler of the fifth, has highly emotional affairs which may be superficial as well as bring trouble and sorrow to the object of affections.

Pluto in Cancer, ruler of the fifth, has a strong need of home and security in order to be fulfilled in a relationship and looks for an idealized or magical love affair.

Leo on the Fifth Cusp

Leo on the fifth house cusp gives purposefulness to love affairs and loves with the aim of having children; the native is egotistic and self-centered in love.

Sun in Leo, ruler of the fifth, is very ambitious in love and fond of children; native overwhelms sweetheart with affection, although in a quiet way.

Moon in Leo, ruler of the fifth, is not a good position, as the native is egotistic in love and has difficulty finding the right kind of sweetheart.

Mercury in Leo, ruler of the fifth, thinks love is secondary, being only the means to an end and is greatly influenced by the opinions of others (aspects are important).

Venus in Leo, ruler of the fifth, is very forthright in opinions about love, loves a good time, attracts strong lovers, and lends permanency to love.

Mars in Leo, ruler of the fifth, is very ardent in love, which is reciprocated, and is generous but severe in love.

Jupiter in Leo, ruler of the fifth, loves wisely and generously, but love is secondary to its objective of marriage.

Saturn in Leo, ruler of the fifth, is ardent but restrained in love and hardly knows how to express himself or herself.

Uranus in Leo, ruler of the fifth indicates constant quarrels and reconciliations unless Mars or Saturn afflicts, meaning that reconciliations do not take place.

Neptune in Leo, ruler of the fifth, has a chaotic love nature due to failure to understand personal emotions; lack of self-control can lead to discredit and disgrace. Loves unwisely, sometimes out of desire for pleasure. Mimicry is an element of the love nature.

Pluto in Leo, ruler of the fifth, brings a need to have personal freedom within a love affair; either extremely selfish or spiritually compassionate.

Virgo on the Fifth Cusp

Virgo on the fifth house cusp sometimes denies a love life due to the native's hypercritical character; love is matter-of-fact rather than sentimental, although inwardly the feelings are deep and strong.

Sun in Virgo, ruler of the fifth, is self-centered and uninterested in love; the native sometimes attempts to express his or her emotional self through mental exercises.

Moon in Virgo, ruler of the fifth, tends to be timid, chaste, and refined.

Mercury in Virgo, ruler of the fifth, has a love instinct that is undeveloped or subordinated to other interests; the native attempts to analyze his love nature (note aspects carefully).

Venus in Virgo, ruler of the fifth, shows love that is often based on pity. This is not a very good position for Venus, as love affairs may be stultified (aspects are important).

Mars in Virgo, ruler of the fifth, shows that self-satisfaction characterizes the native, and he or she may have aversion to love affairs or may have secret love affairs.

Jupiter in Virgo, ruler of the fifth, may indicate celibacy, but note aspects; if love nature is otherwise strong, the native may be entirely dependent on a sweetheart.

Saturn in Virgo, ruler of the fifth, is cold and matter-of-fact and attempts to reduce love to a science.

Uranus in Virgo, ruler of the fifth, is in a position of unusual self-sacrifice and complete surrender to the love nature, there is some danger of looseness in morals (aspects are important).

Neptune in Virgo, ruler of the fifth, gives a position of extremes: this is either very chaste and celibate or the very opposite—a libertine; hence, aspects are very important.

Pluto in Virgo, ruler of the fifth, is arrogant even in romance until the native is purged of egotism. If the native wounds others he will be hurt in return.

Libra on the Fifth Cusp

Libra on the fifth house cusp gives balance to the love life, but there is great fondness for pleasure and attention from the opposite sex.

Sun in Libra, ruler of the fifth, gives a native who demands love and must be in love to be happy.

Moon in Libra, ruler of the fifth, is in a deceptive position, as native appears fickle whereas actually he is sincere but with a strong desire for change, causing each affair to be short.

Mercury in Libra, ruler of the fifth, when unaspected, has a love nature which is not strong; aspects are of the utmost importance.

Venus in Libra, ruler of the fifth, seeks beauty and brings wholesome and refined love.

Mars in Libra, ruler of the fifth, searches actively for love but is brazen and unchaste in his affairs, has strong love affairs that do not culminate in marriage, and is dominated by his or her passions.

Jupiter in Libra, ruler of the fifth, is decorous, orthodox, and very careful in his love affairs which usually culminate in a happy marriage.

Saturn in Libra, ruler of the fifth, is selfish and jealous in love.

Uranus in Libra, ruler of the fifth, is more interested in pleasure than in love; love affairs are short, varied, and changing.

Neptune in Libra, ruler of the fifth, will accept almost any lover. Neptune afflicted in this position could indicate a prostitute; hence aspects are important, for this position may bring licentiousness; they are good actors in love affairs and real life.

Pluto in Libra, ruler of the fifth, creates very special children belonging to various categories; it means rape if badly aspected or birth of a desired child through a surrogate mother or artificial insemination if well aspected.

Scorpio on the Fifth Cusp

Scorpio on the fifth house cusp substitutes sensuality for love, but in a highly developed native the sentimental and emotional nature may be on a high plane. Since the natural desire to procreate is based on love, there is a subtle but close tie between Scorpio and the fifth house which all too frequently expresses itself in sensuality. In all cases note the aspects and sign positions.

Sun in Scorpio, ruler of the fifth, denies children and the love nature is strong but selfish.

Moon in Scorpio, ruler of the fifth, is a very poor position, bringing low company and pleasure as a substitute for love.

Mercury in Scorpio, ruler of the fifth, has love escapades which have a deleterious effect on character; sex dominates the native's mind and his love affairs as well (note aspects).

Venus in Scorpio, ruler of the fifth, means prostitution and low morals (note aspects).

Mars in Scorpio, ruler of the fifth, is arduous and passionate in love, bringing injury to the loved one; he is over-emotional; as well as bringing stability and faithfulness unless afflicted (aspects are important).

Jupiter in Scorpio, ruler of the fifth, causes the native's rashness and hyper-emotionalism which may give rise to very peculiar ideas about love, leading even to the extreme of celibacy (in which event note the aspects of Neptune).

Saturn in Scorpio, ruler of the fifth, brings secret affairs; he or she is ambitious but cold and calculating in love; health may be affected by abuses.

Uranus in Scorpio, ruler of the fifth, has many sexual attachments; however, this often means only a love of the unorthodox, with sex more a mental than physical passion.

Neptune in Scorpio, ruler of the fifth, is a very bad position, indicating danger of venereal infection and excesses in narcotics, alcohol, and other pleasures as a surrogate for normal emotional expression.

Pluto in Scorpio, ruler of the fifth, indicates the possibility and danger of AIDS and other sexually transmitted diseases.

Sagittarius on the Fifth Cusp

Sagittarius on the fifth house cusp causes the native to be demonstratively affectionate, impulsive, and expressive, but the heart is not deeply involved, so the love nature is idealistic.

Sun in Sagittarius, ruler of the fifth, is generous in love, and showers gifts on the lover.

Moon in Sagittarius, ruler of the fifth, often has two love affairs at a time; the native is very susceptible to flattery from the opposite sex.

Mercury in Sagittarius, ruler of the fifth (the aspects are important), when well-aspected, has kindliness and wisdom in coping with his emotional life.

Venus in Sagittarius, ruler of the fifth, is very gentle in love but in danger of dual affairs.

Mars in Sagittarius, ruler of the fifth, is rash in love; but it sometimes brings love at first sight.

Jupiter in Sagittarius, ruler of the fifth, is idealistic and philosophical as well as being generous and outspoken in love.

Saturn in Sagittarius, ruler of the fifth, is self-centered and rides roughshod over others as well as being ambitious in love, but shallow, which brings distress.

Uranus in Sagittarius, ruler of the fifth, has dual attachments but little real love; there is a tendency to promiscuity.

Neptune in Sagittarius, ruler of the fifth, is very imprudent in affairs of the heart.

Pluto in Sagittarius, ruler of the fifth, loves the one he or she is with; love can be fleeting.

Capricorn on the Fifth Cusp

Capricorn on the fifth house cusp makes the native appear cold and calculating; however, the affection, although unromantic and rather matter-of-course, has true depth and the native is extremely faithful.

Sun in Capricorn, ruler of the fifth, is ambitious and materialistic in love and makes love to superiors for financial gain or promotion.

Moon in Capricorn, ruler of the fifth, is moody in love, hypocritical and unscrupulous, and finds affections continually cause difficulties.

Mercury in Capricorn, ruler of the fifth, may be scheming or cunning in love affairs, but has little real feeling (note aspects).

Venus in Capricorn, ruler of the fifth, is fickle in love and has disappointments in love; sometimes this confers a sense of loyalty (aspects should be noted).

Mars in Capricorn, ruler of the fifth, lets parents assume too important a part in the native's love life.

Jupiter in Capricorn, ruler of the fifth, seeks lovers who use relationships to foster their own aims.

Saturn in Capricorn, ruler of the fifth, is calculating and ambitious in love; the threat of disappointment hangs over the native like the sword of Damocles.

Uranus in Capricorn, ruler of the fifth, tends to moral laxity; the native almost always brings trouble to the object of affections.

Neptune in Capricorn, ruler of the fifth, is impractical in love.

Pluto in Capricorn, ruler of the fifth, is cold and controlling, pushing for change.

Aquarius on the Fifth Cusp

Aquarius on the fifth house cusp makes the native idealistic in early love affairs; he or she is easily led and hence misled into unwholesome situations.

Sun in Aquarius, ruler of the fifth, knows that finding a worthy love partner is difficult but, when found, provides a relationship of great happiness.

Moon in Aquarius, ruler of the fifth, brings romantic love affairs; this is usually an excellent position if the native does not have too critical a character.

Mercury in Aquarius, ruler of the fifth, has extensive correspondence with a distant sweetheart; native is often in love with self but more frequently love affairs play an important role in his life.

Venus in Aquarius, ruler of the fifth, may bring long engagement; idealism makes it difficult to find a suitable lover (note aspects).

Mars in Aquarius, ruler of the fifth, brings imprudent love affairs which turn out well; in a feminine chart, this brings devotion from a lover.

Jupiter in Aquarius, ruler of the fifth, is attracted to intellectually superior members of opposite sex.

Saturn in Aquarius, ruler of the fifth, is rather matter-of-fact in love affairs but exceedingly faithful.

Uranus in Aquarius, ruler of the fifth, has conflict between mind and emotions, mentality and feelings, which causes problems in love affairs; carefully note the native's character.

Neptune in Aquarius, ruler of the fifth, seeks idealistic love affairs.

Pluto in Aquarius, ruler of the fifth, brings a wide variety of love affairs, each motivating the native to transform his or her view of love.

Pisces on the Fifth Cusp

Pisces on the fifth house cusp produces the clinging-vine type of lover in the feminine chart and the lackadaisical lover in the male chart—very passive and accepting injuries of all kinds just to be in love.

Sun in Pisces, ruler of the fifth house, is haughty and overbearing (note aspects), for the native may be a love profiteer.

Moon in Pisces, ruler of the fifth, has dreamy, phlegmatic love affairs that may be sensuous; is changeable; and can be sexually perverse.

Mercury in Pisces, ruler of the fifth, has a strong tendency to instability in love affairs, but aspects are of utmost importance.

Venus in Pisces, ruler of the fifth, is usually an excellent position with some idealism and much discretion; the native derives much pleasure from love affairs.

Mars in Pisces, ruler of the fifth is usually a good position indicating passionate love affairs which sometimes involve violence or even cruelty.

Jupiter in Pisces, ruler of the fifth, goes to extremes, either complete chastity and celibacy or a false and parasitic affection.

Saturn in Pisces, ruler of the fifth, becomes involved in love ties that may end tragically and has deprivation of a normal love life.

Uranus in Pisces, ruler of the fifth, has unnatural love and ill-placed affections (aspects are important).

Neptune in Pisces, ruler of the fifth, is idealistic love, as well as romantic disappointment.

Pluto in Pisces, ruler of the fifth, seeks transformation through spiritual love.

The student should be reminded that these are only suggestions as the chart must be studied as a whole to determine the native's character. A complete analysis should be made along the lines set forth in Volume II of this textbook series.

Synthesis in any horoscopic interpretation means weighing values against each other and determining their mutual relations. Practice in horoscopic interpretation develops in the student a keen perception of such relative values, and the application of this perception to interpretation is the key to a correct judgment of the nature and strength of any combination as well as to its probable expression in the native's life.

This is the art of astrology; only by careful and logical treatment of all these factors can any student become a master.

Review Questions for Chapter 7

1. Upon what basis is your present romantic attachment founded? Does this show clearly in both horoscopes?

2. What difference would result from a young man having Saturn in Aquarius as ruler of the fifth house and a youth having Venus in Libra as ruler of the fifth house? Elaborate.

3. What factors would be most likely present in the horoscope of a celibate monk or nun?

4. How would you counsel two 20-year-olds having Sun-Moon conjunctions? Would you look any differently at these same factors in the horoscopes of 40-year-old lovers?

5. Explain the difference between love and marriage in your own words.

| CHAPTER 8 |

MARITAL RELATIONSHIPS

WHILE THE SEVENTH IS THE HOUSE of marriage, there is more to the question than that. House seven dominates the contractual aspect of marriage, but by itself it cannot reveal the basis of the contract, as this is affected by the native's personality, attitude, and character.

One need not be a student of astrology to know that marriage takes place for a number of reasons. On the whole, however, they can be classified into two major groups: one based on the desire for association plus the subconscious urge to procreate and the other based on more materialistic considerations of economic security or social advancement. The latter type of marriage usually occurs later in life than the first type and does not necessarily indicate the same horoscopic factors.

The astrology of marriage has aroused at least as much attention as the astrology of love, perhaps more. And, as with love, much of the relevant astrological literature seems more the product of vague minds seeking public acclaim and self-aggrandizement than based on the hard facts of reason and logic in horoscopic delineation. One of the most commonly encountered fallacies is that the native whose Sun is in an earth sign will get along well in marriage with a spouse whose Sun is in one of the other two earth signs, etc. This has no foundation in fact except to the extent that the Sun in both charts is related to marriage factors in these charts.

An enduring liaison or *union fibre* will often be indicated astrologically as marriage since they presuppose the same relationship between the partners as in marriage, frequently with greater mutual loyalty and devotion. Such unions usually occur after the twenty-eighth birthday rather than before; in other words, they result from indications of late marriage rather than early marriage.

While early marriage usually causes a sudden change in social relations, the establishment of a new home, orange blossoms, and music; late marriages or enduring liaisons are rather the result of a gradual union of the affections into which both partners slip without any upheaval in their mode of life. Late unions are the natural outcome of close association, either in employment or social life.

Marriage undertaken only for social reasons (often found in the charts of royalty where the participants have little opportunity for personal choice) is usually shown in the horoscope as a business partnership. Harmonious factors in the charts of the two partners, and the intimate association of marriage, may bring union of the affections or love at a later date, but these may be entirely absent at the time of marriage. A woman who uses her physical attractions to get a good husband and social position hardly differs at all, astrologically, from the one who uses these same attractions as a profession. The planetary indications will be similar, the main difference being seen in the character, with the element of promiscuity being absent in the native with good character. Likewise, if the woman's horoscope indicates the qualities of housewife and mother, as well as the other elements which enter into the definition of a wife, these will offset any tendencies toward the generally recognized immoral acts.

From time immemorial the Moon and Venus have been the significators of marriage in the masculine horoscope, as the Sun and Mars are in the feminine. The author finds it wise to regard Mars as a sub-influence in the masculine horoscope and Venus as a sub-influence in a feminine chart. It is also very advantageous to consider the ruler of the fifth house, particularly if it is Mars in a masculine horoscope or Venus in a feminine one, as the significator of fifth and seventh houses matters, unless the morality of the chart is so low, and influences for marriage so negative, as to prevent marriage from ever occurring. Some leading European astrologers call this Grant's application of fifth house rulerships.

The wise student will consider similar applications of the ruler of the seventh house cusp in relation to marriage.

In addition to this research and the ancient precepts handed down to us, the native's character is of course fundamental to an interpretation of marriage factors in a horoscope. Everything rests on character and, once this has been studied, the other determinations may be considered: love, marriage, profession, or honor.

The following houses are involved in marriage:

1. House seven for marriage and partnership;

2. House one for the native's relation to marriage; here the Sun-Moon polarity is very important;

3. House five for the love factors in marriage and the native's interest or lack of interest in children;

4. Houses 10 and 11 for the social factors in marriage;

5. Houses 10 and 11 for the economic factors in marriage;

6. The house in which the ruler of house seven is posited.

When these have been ascertained, the indications for likelihood of marriage may be sought. The native will probably marry if the significators are strong in sign and house, especially in the fruitful signs of Cancer, Scorpio, and Pisces; if they are without malefic aspects from Saturn, Neptune, and Pluto; if houses seven and one have fruitful signs on the cusps; and if houses one and seven are free of afflicted malefics. However, even malefics in these houses may not prevent marriage. Saturn in house seven, if weak and badly aspected (particularly by the ruler of the Ascendant or the ruler of house seven), will undoubtedly prevent marriage, but Saturn in house seven without aspect or well-aspected may give marriage to an older person, a widow or widower, a studious person, or a quiet and retiring one. The author does not agree that Saturn in the seventh or first house always prevents marriage. Indeed, Saturn in the seventh house will give great ambition for marriage and may be a stabilizing factor in it.

Marriage will probably be delayed or prevented if the significators are weak, if they afflict each other, if they are in the barren signs (Aries, Gemini, Leo, Virgo, or Capricorn) without any strengthening factors, or if barren signs are on the cusps of the first and seventh houses. Marriage may occur in the absence of favorable indications, or in the presence of ones usually considered unfavorable to marriage for the customary motives, in which case the marriage will count for little in life. This category may include forced marriage.

Early marriage is indicated when the Sun or Moon favorably aspect a fruitful sign and especially when they aspect each other favorably; when many planets are in the eastern half of the chart (excluding house twelve, which sometimes brings secret marriage); and when the Moon is increasing in light plus no unfavorable influence from Saturn. Late marriage is indicated, in an otherwise favorable horoscope, when Saturn is strong or the determining planets are in Saturnian signs. A late marriage may also be caused by the native's idealistic tendencies early in life; for example, if Pisces is on house seven and its ruler, Neptune, is in house nine, the native's idealism about marriage may prevent it. Whenever the ruler of house seven is found in house nine, the native looks for an ideal spouse. In considering marriageable age the native's social customs and racial background must be taken into account, as in some cases the parents still select the marriage partner, even in the United States. Likewise, in certain social strata of some countries marriage rarely takes place before the twenty-fifth birthday.

Probability of more than one marriage is indicated (if there are any marriage indications at all) when double-bodied signs are on the first or seventh cusps and especially if Gemini and Sagittarius, or the indicators of marriage, are in double-bodied signs. This probability is increased by malefic indications in house seven or if the marriage significator is afflicted, particularly by Uranus or Mars. Likelihood of more than one marriage is also indicated by two or more planets in house seven when there is not a fixed sign on the cusp or unless one of these planets is Saturn. The author has found that, in masculine horoscopes, Uranus square the Moon brings divorce or separation from the wife. This separation, if other factors corroborate, may be due to conditions beyond their control such as the profession taking the husband away from home and family. Uranus square the Sun in a feminine horoscope almost inevitably brings divorce or separation from the husband.

Certain ancient rules have been handed down concerning the character and description of the marriage partner, but in the twentieth century, when women have the same freedom of choice as men, the partner is less easy to determine that the rules would seem to indicate.

First, the native's character must be remembered. Then the following rules may be helpful. Note carefully the positions of Sun and Moon in the natal horoscope. According to ancient tradition the marriage partner is indicated by the first aspect made by the Moon as it moves forward in the zodiac, whether the aspect be favorable or unfavorable. The strength of the aspect is important, however: while a sextile is not as strong as a conjunction, the luminary's progression by sextile to a planet in houses five, seven, or eleven would naturally be more indicative than conjunction with a planet in houses two, six, or twelve.

This rule has been opposed on the ground that the Sun would never aspect the Sun by progression in a feminine horoscope, as an indicator, before aspecting some other planet; yet many women marry men who are ruled by the Sun. This argument is of little value, however, because if the Sun's first aspect were to a planet in Leo, the partner would be strongly leonine (solar) in character. The sign containing the significator definitely indicates the character of the individual chosen as marriage partner while being modified by the nature of the planet involved and the character of the aspect, as well as by natal aspects shown to that planet. The house in which the significator is posited will indicate the circumstances of meeting.

Competent astrologers contend that in applying these rules only aspects of a progressed luminary to a progressed (and not natal) planet should be considered. According to our experience this is not necessarily true, as the aspect will often be the same whether to a progressed or natal position. But in those cases where it is not, the Sun's or Moon's progression forward in the zodiac to an aspect with a natal planet is the true significator of the marriage partner's character, nature, disposition, and physical appearance.

An analysis of these ancient rules will show that they are not special rules at all but merely logical deductions from normal expectations when rulerships of luminaries are considered. The Sun represents all the men influencing a woman's life generally, while the Moon indicates the influence of the opposite sex on a man. Thus the author's old adage holds true, that rules are given only to direct the student's thinking into certain broad channels.

Eighteenth-century astrologers developed another method for determining the character and qualities of the marriage partner. It is derived from practice in horary astrology and is given here only for the sake of completeness, but it is a method worth investigating. The house in which the significator of the marriage partner is found becomes the Ascendant of the proposed partner's horoscope, and the influence of the planets is read according to their changed house positions. While this provides some illuminating detail, the author regards its use as justified only when the luminary application is so striking as to indicate very strong influence of the marriage partner on the native's life.

The use of marriage horoscopes is becoming more and more common in astrological practice, since it is recognized that the family unit commences in the horoscope with the pronouncement of marriage. A chart cast for this moment and place is the true birth chart of the family as a social unit and, when considering connection with the charts of the marriage partners, is of great benefit for interpreting the family's life. Being related to the horoscopes of both husband and wife, it will necessarily amplify their natal charts as related to each other. Leading American astrologers have used such charts to advantage in determining the birth times of children and the whole development of family life. Further research along these lines will doubtless prove beneficial, since marriage is not (usually) easily broken when once undertaken. In such a chart the Ascendant represents the husband and house VII the wife.

Signs and Planets in the Seventh House

A brief tabulation of signs and planets in the seventh house is presented. These are just suggestions and are to be used only as a key to correct interpretation.

Aries on the Seventh Cusp

Aries on the seventh cusp frequently brings marital unhappiness due to incompatibility. If this is a very strong house in a feminine chart, the woman will try to dominate.

Sun in Aries in the seventh gives an energetic marriage

partner; in a feminine chart, the husband will be well-to-do.

Moon in Aries in the seventh tends to secretiveness on the part of both husband and wife.

Mercury in Aries in the seventh is anxiety about marriage; the native makes a great effort to marry early.

Venus in Aries in the seventh indicates an early liaison.

Mars in Aries in the seventh shows intimacies before marriage.

Jupiter in Aries in the seventh is an ambitious and sometimes reckless partner.

Saturn in Aries in the seventh shows jealousies in marriage; aspects are important.

Uranus in Aries in the seventh indicates that the marriage union may terminate suddenly.

Neptune in Aries in the seventh means that aspects are important: if good, marriage is over-intense; if bad, mutual incompatibility and trouble.

Pluto in Aries in the seventh shows control issues, and sometimes abuse.

Taurus on the Seventh Cusp

Taurus on the seventh cusp usually brings wealth in marriage and a proud marriage partner.

Sun in Taurus in the seventh means partners follow their own ways, but marriage is successful.

Moon in Taurus in the seventh says the native leads a dual life.

Mercury in Taurus in the seventh shows infidelity due to excessive curiosity.

Venus in Taurus in the seventh means, in feminine horoscopes, being too pleasure-loving for monogamy; in a male chart the wife spends too much money on pleasure.

Mars in Taurus in the seventh gives strife; the marriage relationship is tragic, often through domination of marriage partner.

Jupiter in Taurus in the seventh means that marriage is stable and honorable.

Saturn in Taurus in the seventh means marriage brings on financial difficulties.

Uranus in Taurus in the seventh brings sudden rupture of marriage as well as a bossy partner.

Neptune in Taurus in the seventh brings a marriage partner who is languorous but deceitful.

Pluto in Taurus in the seventh indicates a marriage partner with an unbending nature and a desire to control marital issues.

Gemini on the Seventh Cusp

Gemini on house seventh cusp usually brings more than one marriage, one of which is generally late in life.

Sun in Gemini in the seventh means marriage upsets equanimity, no inner peace, and partner is a gossip.

Moon in Gemini in the seventh is not a good position in the male chart, bringing curious marital relations such as having a mistress rather than a wife; in both male and female charts it brings marital relations without marriage.

Mercury in Gemini in the seventh means a native neglects marital responsibilities; definitely indicates two marriages, with the first often ending in divorce.

Venus in Gemini in the seventh gives mutual infidelity; the native is demonstratively affectionate toward partner.

Mars in Gemini in the seventh means much bickering and quarreling in marriage.

Jupiter in Gemini in the seventh gives a happy marriage

with partners well adjusted to one another.

Saturn in Gemini in the seventh means marriage to a studious or quiet person or to an older person or one far from home.

Uranus in Gemini in the seventh gives unconventional ideas with little regard for marriage.

Neptune in Gemini in the seventh means marriage to a foreigner or marriage abroad as well as a peculiar attachment to mother.

Pluto in Gemini in the seventh gives a marriage full of struggles, often ending with separation for the purpose of new liaison; the nature must beware of eloping with a younger mate.

Cancer on the Seventh Cusp

Cancer on the seventh cusp can bring difficulty in marriage through demands for sentimental expression. Note the position of the Moon.

Sun in Cancer in the seventh means the marriage gradually deteriorates and ends in estrangement.

Moon in Cancer in the seventh means marriage comes early in life to a partner with developed maternal instinct but changeable in affections.

Mercury in Cancer in the seventh demands praise and is susceptible to flattery from partner.

Venus in Cancer in the seventh is highly sentimental and emotional, not to be trusted away from partner.

Mars in Cancer in the seventh is danger of scandal in marriage (note the aspects).

Jupiter in Cancer in the seventh is a marriage that brings social advance, some secret in marriage, and, if afflicted, the marital partner could be sickly.

Saturn in Cancer in the seventh has a great urge for marriage but tends to establish only friendly or platonic relationships.

Uranus in Cancer in the seventh means elopement and hasty marriage.

Neptune in Cancer in the seventh says marriage is unsatisfactory, flabby, and fluid; and partner is the dreamy type.

Pluto in Cancer in the seventh welcomes a strong partner even when they are adversaries, has inflamed passions early in the marriage with possible suicide later, and needs the security of legalized unions.

Leo on the Seventh Cusp

Leo on the seventh house cusp lends dignity to marriage and to partner; partner may rule or dominate marriage.

Sun in Leo in the seventh means a marriage to a social climber or the native himself may desire social advancement through marriage.

Moon in Leo in the seventh brings a proud partner; husband and wife both lead their own lives.

Mercury in Leo in the seventh is too much influenced in marriage by appearance and opinions of partner.

Venus in Leo in the seventh expects luxury from marriage and tends to be jealous.

Mars in Leo in the seventh, oddly enough, brings much happiness in marriage if partners are of about the same age; and there is much activity in the marriage state.

Jupiter in Leo in the seventh means marriage to a wealthy person or to a friend of the family.

Saturn in Leo in the seventh gives a partner who is ambitious and jealous.

Uranus in Leo in the seventh is dictatorial toward partner;

small differences are magnified and lead to divorce.

Neptune in Leo in the seventh gives chaos in marriage and brings separation for reasons not clearly understood.

Pluto in Leo in the seventh is impersonal where affection is *needed,* too stubborn to release another from vows, jealous, and unfaithful.

Virgo on the Seventh Cusp

Virgo on the seventh house cusp brings restraint in marital relationship, little romance but acceptance of marriage as a duty, and the native makes great efforts to ensure partner's happiness but is really better off unmarried. Note Mercury's position and aspects.

Sun in Virgo in the seventh gives a marriage functioning more out of sense of duty than desire.

Moon in Virgo in the seventh means a marriage which brings remorse and regret.

Mercury in Virgo in the seventh, when afflicted, brings marriage to a nagging person; when well aspected, to a precise and orderly person with a good intellect; marriage is more a matter of intellect than of the emotions.

Venus in Virgo in the seventh means partner is from an inferior social station.

Mars in Virgo in the seventh gives a marriage partner who brings unhappiness and grief.

Jupiter in Virgo in the seventh marries to please parents.

Saturn in Virgo in the seventh means happiness through marriage to an older person.

Uranus in Virgo in the seventh indicates many difficult conditions in the home which are cleverly handled.

Neptune in Virgo in the seventh is a strong urge for early

marriage which brings many disappointments unless aspects are strongly favorable.

Pluto in Virgo in the seventh needs to make a wise choice of partners, can often fill the role of serving the mate, and seeks many acquaintances which seldom works out as desired.

Libra on the Seventh Cusp

Libra on the seventh house cusp gives great desire for marriage.

Unless Venus is badly aspected, the native chooses an excellent partner with emotional balance.

Sun in Libra in the seventh means an excellent marriage, but some danger of separation.

Moon in Libra in the seventh gives a partner who finds marriage very unsatisfactory but remains married through innate demand for companionship.

Mercury in Libra in the seventh means a very matter-of-fact and ordinary marriage.

Venus in Libra in the seventh is almost the ideal position if unafflicted, giving domesticity, great affection, and love of children.

Mars in Libra in the seventh means the partner is energetic and may be oversexed.

Jupiter in Libra in the seventh almost always brings wealth or a dowry and is a fine position for fidelity and mutual understanding.

Saturn in Libra in the seventh is too much egoism in marriage. Uranus in Libra in the seventh means too easy a marriage will bring outside liaisons; difficulties must arise to make partner worthy.

Neptune in Libra in the seventh means the partner is neglectful and lazy.

Pluto in Libra in the seventh struggles for power in marriage, is more suited for counseling than living a relationship, and makes frequent enemies of in-laws.

Scorpio on the Seventh Cusp

Scorpio on seventh house cusp imposes too great demands on the partner; seldom can much happiness be found and the positions of Pluto and Mars are important here.

Sun in Scorpio in the seventh shows treachery toward partner.

Moon in Scorpio in the seventh means married life is vulgar and coarse.

Mercury in Scorpio in the seventh brings separation and estrangement.

Venus in Scorpio in the seventh means marriage to a widow or widower and native will probably outlive partner.

Mars in Scorpio in the seventh delights in making partner unhappy and aspects are important.

Jupiter in Scorpio in the seventh means wealth in marriage but little happiness.

Saturn in Scorpio in seventh brings separation and divorce with native as defendant.

Uranus in Scorpio in the seventh is unpredictable in marriage which usually ends in divorce or separation.

Neptune in Scorpio in the seventh means separation or substance abuse.

Pluto in Scorpio in the seventh means estrangement, divorce, or physical or mental abuse.

Sagittarius on the Seventh Cusp

Sagittarius on the seventh house cusp brings a generous and good-hearted partner, the native is easily consoled in marriage, and there is a strong probability of multiple marriages. Note the position of Jupiter.

Sun in Sagittarius in the seventh means marriage improves the native's social position.

Moon in Sagittarius in the seventh means two marriages are certain, the native is susceptible to flattery, and is easily influenced by partner's appeals to his or her vanity.

Mercury in Sagittarius in the seventh usually brings early marriage and one of native's marriages will bring culture into home life.

Venus in Sagittarius in the seventh means first marriage usually is unhappy through being too early and on poor foundation, but the second marriage is very happy.

Mars in Sagittarius in the seventh means some discord in the home is instigated by the native more than by the partner, but on the whole the home life is energetic and happy.

Saturn in Sagittarius in the seventh indicates divorce or separation through negligence of native and instigated against him or her.

Jupiter in Sagittarius in the seventh gives great harmony and much wealth in the marital state.

Uranus in Sagittarius in the seventh gives instability in marriage, partner dictates and native plays around, and native's attitude toward partner fluctuates.

Neptune in Sagittarius in the seventh means early death of partner.

Pluto in Sagittarius in the seventh means little interest in relationship longevity and constancy.

Capricorn on the Seventh Cusp

Capricorn on the seventh house cusp gives the ability to make the most of marriage and overcome all obstacles.

Sun in Capricorn in the seventh means much display in marriage and a tendency to keep up with the Jones.

Moon in Capricorn in the seventh means the native neglects the partner.

Mercury in Capricorn in the seventh regards marriage as a duty to be fulfilled, not a state to which he should aspire.

Venus in Capricorn in the seventh means the marriage partner is cold and indifferent but loyal.

Mars in Capricorn in the seventh gives much connivance to bring about marriage for a social gain as well as some secrecy about marriage.

Jupiter in Capricorn in the seventh means wealth in marriage but little happiness; marriage is rather matter-of-fact.

Saturn in Capricorn in the seventh means a marriage based on practicality rather than on emotion.

Uranus in Capricorn in the seventh gives separation or divorce.

Neptune in Capricorn in the seventh brings a spiritual connection or one where substance abuse brings hardship.

Pluto in Capricorn in the seventh indicates strife and hardship with the marriage partner, who is difficult at best.

Aquarius on the Seventh Cusp

Aquarius on the seventh house cusp brings much uncertainty to marriage. The native is rather independent, and the marriage partner will be the same; hence danger of a personality clash.

Sun in Aquarius in the seventh means early marriage which often ends in separation or divorce.

Moon in Aquarius in the seventh gives much romance in the marriage or outside it.

Mercury in Aquarius in the seventh means absence or separation for reasons outside the partners' control which does not lead to estrangement.

Venus in Aquarius in the seventh delays marriage but brings happiness to it.

Mars in Aquarius in the seventh means the native should not marry as more happiness will be found in attachments outside marriage.

Jupiter in Aquarius in seventh is an ideal position for marriage if one of pure love.

Saturn in Aquarius in the seventh means much practicality in marriage, but romance as well as a good marriage.

Uranus in Aquarius in the seventh is a marriage of extremes: either a very close union between partners or extreme separation.

Neptune in Aquarius in the seventh could be the ideal marriage or a union with someone odd.

Pluto in Aquarius in the seventh is a marriage partner who feels the need for freedom within the union.

Pisces on the Seventh Cusp

Pisces on the seventh house cusp means Neptune must be well aspected or house seven must be influenced by benefic planets for marriage to be successful.

Sun in Pisces in the seventh brings wealth but unhappiness.

Moon in Pisces in the seventh means drinking or drug addiction in the home; an evil position, as every phase of marriage will be dominated by emotions rather than reason.

Mercury in Pisces in the seventh means everything depends on the position of Neptune and aspects of Mercury.

Venus in Pisces in the seventh means home life is either too gay or else lazy and sensuous.

Mars in Pisces in the seventh brings danger in marriage.

Jupiter in Pisces in the seventh means the partner leans too heavily on native's relatives, especially in a male chart; if afflicted there is dishonesty in marriage.

Saturn in Pisces in the seventh gives much difficulty and trouble in marriage with many unnecessary responsibilities.

Uranus in Pisces in the seventh means separation and divorce.

Neptune in Pisces in the seventh means the tie between the two partners is vague and tenuous, with much confusion.

Pluto in Pisces in the seventh brings a lack of understanding, care, and support between the partners.

Use these suggestions from the viewpoint of analysis, and as starting points of study that can be changed by the chart as a whole. Note all aspects of the ruler of the seventh house ruler as well as the sign and house in which it is posited. These modifying influences can overcome the basic qualities indicated by seventh house positions. Good readings depend upon care and experience, and the primary objective is to help the client avoid or solve problems by knowing the cause.

Review Questions for Chapter 8

1. Which houses are involved in a marriage or longstanding affair? And how?

2. Is an early marriage different from a later one?

3. What indicates more than one marriage during a lifetime?

4. How does the sign on your seventh house suggest you will react in a legal liaison?

5. Are the planets in your seventh house well placed and well aspected? What does this suggest? If there are problems, how can you avoid them or work them out?

|Chapter 9|

Vocational Relationships

Synthesis of the apparently contradictory influences in a chart is as complicated as the life which the chart reflects. This challenge can be met and surmounted only by the application of logic and reason to all astrological problems.

As previously indicated, most of the astrologer's clients seek counsel in one of several major areas; hence three major syntheses should be made of every horoscope. These are health, disease, love, marriage, children, travel, vocation, and financial outlook.

Again it must be emphasized that the first step in reaching a proper determination is to ascertain the native's character as a whole. Any other approach rests on insecure foundations. Thus, while a horoscope may show great money-making ability, if the character is such that the native runs afoul of the law early in life, an opportunity to make money may not present itself. Emotional instability may direct the energies into wrong channels, thus so severely impairing the ability to make money or retain it as to negate otherwise excellent astrological indications.

But this has been repeated so often in earlier chapters that no further discussion is needed.

Profession and Occupation

These matters are extremely important, especially in the horoscopes of children, and wise parents seek guidance here early in their children's lives. If the child's horoscope is correctly delineated, hidden talents can be revealed, wholesome interests stimulated, improper tendencies curbed, and character developed so as to derive the greatest satisfaction from a particular vocation or profession. This is the task of the sincere astrologer.

While an entire course of study could be devoted to this subject also, certain basic principles that have been tested in the fire of experience can be laid down.

Always remember that the planets are more important for profession and occupation than are the signs or the houses. Indeed, this is true for all astrological delineation since the planet represents the primary force while the signs and houses are the qualities and channels of that force. Hence the same general principles of astrological delineation are also to be applied here: learning the nature of the planet, the signification of the sign, and the meaning of the house to which attention is directed. With all of this in mind, the following seven basic rules are to be followed in considering vocation or occupation:

1. House 10: Look at planets in house 10, the ruler of house 10, the houses ruled by planets in house 10, the house and sign in which the ruler of house 10 is found, and finally the influence of any planets aspecting these planets.

2. House 6: Look at planets in house 6, the ruler of house VI, the houses ruled by planets in house 6, the house and sign in which the ruler of house VI is found, and finally the influence of any planets aspecting these planets. House VI, however, relates more to subordinate positions and work of a menial nature.

3. The Sun: Look at the Sun's position both by sign and house, the house which it rules, and all solar aspects (particularly the planet rising just ahead of the Sun). The planet rising ahead

of the Sun (disregarding retrograde motion) applies ultimately to a conjunction with the Sun, but this planet's sign and house positions must be carefully noted. Whether the Sun is oriental or occidental in the horoscope is unimportant.

4. Mercury: Look at its sign and house position together with its aspects. Mercury will often be the planet rising ahead of the Sun because of its proximity to the Sun at all times.

5. The Moon: Look at not the Moon itself, unless it is specifically associated with vocation in the individual horoscope, but the planet which most strongly aspects the Moon, together with this planet's sign and house position.

6. The ruler of the Ascendant: Look carefully its sign and house position as well as aspects.

7. The ruler of the horoscope: Look at the strongest planet in the chart, which is frequently the ruler of the Ascendant. Note its sign and house positions as well as aspects.

Planets as Professions

According to Ptolemy, the two significators of occupation are the planet nearest the Sun and rising before it, plus the strongest planet in the Midheaven. To this modern astrologers have added Mercury, which seems wise. Whole volumes have been written about vocational astrology, but certain general principles can be isolated.

Sun represents executive and administrative positions, in fact, all positions of authority; bankers, particularly in investment banking; speculators in securities; goldsmiths, jewelers; and self-employed businessmen.

Moon represents positions dealing with the general public; positions involving much travel; real estate and liquor dealers; restaurant and tavern operators; nurses; and if the chart otherwise indicates a practitioner of the healing arts, the specialized field of obstetrics.

Mercury represents all forms of clerical employment; bookkeeping and accountancy; sales; fulfillment; architects; buyers; customer service representatives; linguists; reporters; and, if the chart otherwise indicates a practitioner of the healing arts, a specialist in psychiatry, neurology, or dermatology (the last especially if Venus is also prominent).

Venus represents all vocations demanding an artistic touch, such as interior decorating; gardening; women's apparel; adornment; artists; musicians; singing; acting; and, if the chart otherwise indicates a practitioner of the healing arts, a specialist in eye, ear, nose, and throat or a dermatologist.

Mars represents mechanics; machinists; soldiers; workers with cutting tools; workers in metal, especially iron and steel; pugilists; policemen; firemen; and, if the chart otherwise indicates a practitioner of the healing arts, a surgeon or dental surgeon.

Jupiter represents lawyers; clergymen; vocations having to do with outdoor sports; wholesaling: editors or publishers; security salesman; if the chart otherwise indicates a practitioner of the healing arts, a specialist in cancer, chiropody, or institutional medicine; vocations having to do with money handling such as cashier or bank teller, and philosophers.

Saturn represents all vocations having to do with land, farming, building, construction, or contracting; the mechanics of small instruments such as watches, clocks, chronometers and microscopes; if the chart otherwise indicates a practitioner of the healing arts, a bone specialist or osteopath; research workers; and advertising specialists.

Uranus represents all scientific pursuits; invention; automobile and aircraft manufacture and operation; X-ray and electrical work; vocations having to do with air; utility companies; if the chart otherwise indicates a practitioner of the healing arts, an X-ray specialist or chiropractor; astrologers; and archeologists.

Neptune represents all vocations having to do with liquids such as oil or water; distillers; oil-well operators; the navy; gas station operators; institutional work in hospitals, jails, homes for children and the aged, or mental hospitals; photographers; and, if the chart otherwise indicates a practitioner of the healing arts, a specialist in anesthesia, nursing, or institutional medicine.

Pluto represents metallurgists; miners; plumbers; detectives; cave explorers; geologists; psychologists and social workers; antique dealers; magicians; and submarine specialists.

Signs as Professions

While the signs are subsidiary in importance to the planets, the general influence of the signs can be summarized as follows:

Aries represents employment requiring much activity; pioneering; the army; cattle dealing; veterinary surgeon; and, when combined with Gemini, teaching.

Taurus represents real estate agents and brokers; gardeners; wood merchants; and employment in a financial institution.

Gemini represents writers; public relations representatives; librarians; media personnel.

Cancer represents sailors; grocery work; bartenders; caterers; housekeepers; and interior decorators.

Leo represents actors; artists; jockeys; government work at a high level; and administrative positions generally.

Virgo represents clerical work; accounting; printing; chemistry; nursing; governess; guardianship and clothes dealers.

Libra represents assayer; bank clerk; broker; designer; and legal work in a subordinate capacity.

Scorpio represents surgeons; photographer; metal worker; and the navy.

Sagittarius represents explorers; lawyers; clergy; physicians; horse and cattle dealers; welfare workers; and occult interests.

Capricorn represents advertising; political work; diplomats; administrations; and farming.

Aquarius represents electricians; aviators; scientists; promoters; inventors; architects; and sculptors.

Pisces represents fishermen; hospital attendants; prison guards; nurses; authors; brewers; sailors; and odd-job workers.

Triplicities as Professions

If planets are grouped in a given triplicity, and that triplicity is angular in the chart, success may be along the lines thus indicated. Triplicity influences may be summarized as follows:

Earth signs mean manual labor; mining; farming; and everything that has to do with the earth.

Water signs mean work with fluids; sailors; brewers; bartenders; chemists; painters; and industries having to do with textiles and fabrics.

Fire signs mean surgeon; mechanic; soldier; and everything that has to do with creative employment and industry.

Air signs mean all vocations of an intellectual nature; literature; the arts; and the intellectual sciences.

Quadruplicities as Professions

Similarly, if planets are grouped in a given quadruplicity that dominates the angles in the chart, vocation will be affected thereby. The following suggestions are pertinent:

Cardinal signs are administrative positions; managers; directors, pioneers, trade; and positions in which native make things happen.

Fixed signs are employment with established concerns; manufacturing; and producing companies.

Mutable signs mean a better servant than master; agent; commercial traveler; speaker; and uniformed position.

Astrologers will frequently be asked about changing the position or vocation, as the individual may be dissatisfied with his present job. In such cases, the horoscope must be progressed, since the potentialities of the natal chart will be insufficient. Take into account environmental factors, the native's age, and his academic background, while applying to these his reason and practical sense.

The foregoing will provide the student with valuable clues, but caution must be exercised at all times for in no other field of astrology can error lead to such unsatisfactory results. A child must not be raised to be a doctor, lawyer, or minister of the gospel simply because that was his father's vocation. His own natural aptitudes and abilities must be determine; their utilization will bring him greater contentment whatever his vocation may be. Ancient rules may be more easily discarded in this branch of astrology than in others, for the advance of civilization has altered environment and opportunity, and today the lowliest can become the greatest.

Wealth and Finance

Material well-being is closely allied with vocation, and financial wealth is simply material well-being correctly utilized. In one case wealth may bring catastrophe or distress, in another pleasure and the opportunity to serve mankind. Again, character is vital.

Many small favorable factors in the horoscope of a careful and thrifty person might yield far greater material promise than the chart of an extravagant or generous person, although the latter might find greater contentment in life. A retiring and timorous person will not recognize opportunities which will be seized by the courage and aggressive native. The complex of factors indicating financial success in a foreign land will have little meaning in a horoscope indicating that the native will always remain close to his place of birth.

Planets as Wealth

Each planet has some relationship to money through sign and house position, but some planets seem to have influence regardless of position. The following suggestions may be useful:

Sun brings position and wealth and love of display; the native is extravagant to keep up appearances.

Moon brings popularity and sometimes fame so money comes from activities dealing directly with the public.

Mercury, by itself, has little to do with money, so aspects are of primary importance. It may indicate gain through intellectual pursuits but, when afflicted by Venus, Mars, Saturn, Jupiter, or Neptune, either poor judgment or dishonesty is indicated.

Venus, when angular or well-aspected, indicates not only money but a life of ease, often acquired through others or by marriage.

Mars influence on money is indirect except when the chart shows Mars to have influence by position. It indicates the energy and driving force needed to acquire money but also frequently indicates extravagance.

Jupiter, when angular and well-aspected, the great benefic, is always a sign of wealth and even its afflictions, unless very great, do not tend to poverty.

Saturn tends to thrift and sometimes to miserliness. When well aspected, it favors slow gains and accumulation by saving and gives ambition and patient determination. But Saturn afflictions frequently indicate poverty.

Uranus, unless prominent in the specific chart, has little to do with money directly; it can bring sudden losses but also unexpected gifts.

Neptune resembles Uranus in having little to do with money directly unless such a relationship is indicated by chart position; however, evil aspects to Neptune often cause ruin.

Pluto brings a desire for the power which money gives and may be tempted to obtain riches through dishonest means.

Houses as Wealth

The even-numbered houses—two, four, six, eight, ten, and twelve—have a more direct connection with money than the odd-numbered houses. Here the underlying logic of astrology becomes manifest: the odd-numbered houses are the masculine, aggressive, outgoing avenues of life, while the even-numbered are the feminine, passive, receptive avenues. Even though all houses in the chart have some association with money, a consideration of the even-numbered houses will show why their influence is greater:

The second house represents money and finances in itself, and the planets in it will naturally indicate how money is gained or lost. Similarly, the house and sign position of the second house ruler is important, as its strength or debility will be a determining factor.

The fourth house represents property, especially land and buildings. Saturn's relationship to this house is very important and, if the chart is calculated accurately for time of birth, aspects to the cusp of house four should be considered. As this house has much to do with old age, a favorable fourth house usually indicates economic security and ease in old age.

The sixth house has to do with both employment and employees (the trinities and quadrants will serve to indicate which is dominant). The Sun in strong relation to house 6 indicates the employer, the self-employed man, as will also the ruler of the Ascendant but to a lesser degree. Contrariwise, the Moon is more indicative of the employee.

House eight relates to money received through the marriage partner, contracts, and inheritances. This house must always be considered in delineation of the second house for money, as well as the seventh house for marriage, and the fourth for old age.

The tenth house is associated with vocation or profession as well as social position and honors which may come to the native. It has less to do with money than with success, but if money is incidental to success, it will be shown here. If the house is strong and the money planets are weak, it may mean fame without fortune; if the house is weak, and the money planets are strong, it may mean fortune without fame. In a feminine chart, however, this house has much to do with social position, especially if marriage significators are strong in relation to it.

The twelfth house indicates restrictions on fortune, the negation of fortune, ruin, and loss. If this house is unduly strong or has a stellium in it, loss of fortune is indicated.

Excellent aspects for money are a trine or sextile of Jupiter to the Moon or Venus, while the same results through thrift and saving may be indicated by a trine or sextile of Saturn to the Moon or Venus. Good aspects of the Sun to Jupiter, the Moon, Venus, or Saturn are fortunate, but waste may also be indicated in the case of the first three bodies. Jupiter with Uranus is better for wealth than Jupiter with Venus, for the latter produces emotional instability. Saturn and the Moon in good aspect favor thrift, saving, and accumulation of wealth, but alone they are of little value; Saturn and Moon must be assisted by the money planets, as otherwise there may be lack of enterprise or avarice.

The influence of a money planet for wealth is greatly increased if it is favorably aspected in a money house or rules the sign on the cusp of that house. Its nature must be judged by the planet, the sign, and the house, but harmonious aspects are essential. Even Jupiter or Venus in the second house, if afflicted, are less fortunate than Mercury or Saturn there when well aspected. The planets in themselves have such definite characters, and the meanings of the houses are so specific and distinct, that a careful financial synthesis is not likely to go far astray.

The first, fifth, and eleventh houses have a more important secondary influence on money than the other odd houses.

The first house indicates the native's personality and attitude toward money; house five relates to speculation and gambling; and house eleven to financial assistance from friends—not only in the form of loans, but also assistance in the form of recommendations, advice and encouragement.

Of course, the Sun and Moon are also to be considered as secondary factors in monetary affairs, being favorable or unfavorable according to position (whether in money houses or aspected to money planets). The Sun is of greater importance in a feminine horoscope and the Moon in a masculine one.

Signs as Wealth

The following list of the influences of the various signs may provide useful clues and suggestions in respect of money matters. While the second house is the primary money house, the significance of these signs in the other money houses will be modified by the planets in them.

Aries in the second house indicates wealth gained by the native's own abilities, either through work or cleverness. Saturn here gives acquisitiveness and ease toward the end of life, if well aspected, Jupiter tends to foreign investments. Mars indicates private means. Venus favors legacies from women or from the mother's side of the family.

Taurus in the second house favors gain through investment or marriage and the native is economical. Venus brings money through the profession. Mars makes the native persevering and ambitious; Jupiter is good for speculation if not badly aspected. Saturn gives industriousness with slow returns.

Gemini in the second house tends to fluctuating finances but usually produces several simultaneous sources of income. Venus brings help from relatives and close friends. Mars indicates that the native may live by his wits (note aspects carefully). Jupiter gives the native ingenuity in finding well-paying positions. Saturn may give a tendency to be tricky in financial matters.

Cancer in the second house causes a person to be careful about finances, economical and thrifty; the native gains through travel or affairs having to do with water. Venus brings income from theaters, public amusements, and pleasure resorts, often having to do with restaurants. Mars brings money through dealings with employees and servants. Jupiter indicates benefits from land and buildings. Saturn delays income and arouses obstacles to the favor of the public.

Leo in the second house favors money through public work or government employment and sometimes indicates wealth; it nearly always brings an attachment to some important employer. Venus here often indicates legacies. Mars gives excellent administrative ability which brings financial gain; the native is active in his work and heads up some important undertaking. Jupiter brings money through land and mining. Saturn often provides government employment, but slow promotions.

Virgo in the second house is good for money from some foreign source, also for navigation and minor positions involving close attention to detail. Venus here can bring losses through a partner. Mars in this position helps to make and lose money. Jupiter brings income through religion or law and may also indicate monetary dealings on a minor scale. Saturn here brings money through association with older people.

Libra in the second house brings money through associations, partnerships, and marriage. Venus here brings money through marriage. Mars causes losses through inferiors. Jupiter brings gains through inferiors. Saturn does not favor wealth, but a satisfactory income is acquired by hard work.

Scorpio in the second house is often a good sign for speculation or for the type of business which brings gain through rapid turnover; the native gains through others' losses. Venus gets the native into secret and doubtful ventures. Mars brings gain through marriage. Jupiter brings losses in all small-scale matters. Saturn here brings money through insurance companies.

Sagittarius in the second house is good for both legacies and speculation, but the native tends to devote his efforts to other than monetary gain. Venus here brings money through vocations involving women and amusements (but more the serious kind of amusement). Mars is good for money through speculation. Jupiter gives lack of interest in money as such, even though it comes rather easily without any concentration by the native. Saturn in this position means that any results are obtained through hard work.

Capricorn in the second house is the business sign, bringing money through advertising. It is a good sign for slowly building up a fortune, but there is danger of miserliness. Venus sometimes causes marriage for money; it brings about partnerships, but the partner gains more than the native (unless Venus is afflicted by the Moon, in which case the reverse is true). Mars brings money through secretive, and sometimes unlawful, procedures. Jupiter gives a sound commercial sense, good for money-making. Saturn gives some danger of avarice and cheating, but the native is primarily interested in money for himself.

Aquarius in the second house is essentially a money sign for corporations, bringing financial success from transport (especially by air) as well as from new and original ventures involving inventions. Venus here is excellent for the higher kind of business. Mars often brings sudden loss. Jupiter brings money from unexpected sources. Saturn brings good financial return from persistent effort along original lines.

Pisces in the second house is a parasitic sign as regards money; the native rarely has the initiative to launch and conduct an enterprise without depending on others. Venus brings money through others, but the native tends to be a sycophant. Marts of ten brings money through dishonest methods. Jupiter gives ingenuity in extracting money from others. Saturn impairs the judgment on money matters.

Ruler of the Second House

The habit should be acquired of looking at the house position of the planet ruling the house of finance and also at the houses in which the rulers of the sixth and tenth houses are found. The ruler of the second house in the various houses brings monetary gain or loss as follows:

Ruler of the second in the first gives gain through the native's own initiative and energy.

Ruler of the second in the second gives wealth, especially when well-aspected, great wealth when well aspected by the ruler of the Ascendant.

Ruler of the second in the third gives gain or loss through relatives, writing, or travel.

Ruler of the second in the fourth gives a good or bad position for old age, depending upon strength and aspects, except when Mars rules house the second.

Ruler of the second in the fifth gives gain or loss through speculation and children are generally well-to-do.

Ruler of the second in the sixth gives gain or loss through servants but possible heavy expenditure on health.

Ruler of the second in the seventh gives loss through marriage partner unless very well-aspected (especially so if in Aries, Scorpio, or Capricorn).

Ruler of the second in the eighth gives gain through legacies and marriage.

Ruler of the second in the ninth gives gain through voyages or navigation and success at some distance from place of birth.

Ruler of the second in the tenth gives gain through a profession or from association with the well-to-do.

Ruler of the second in the eleventh gives gain or loss through friends and organizations.

Ruler of the eighth in the twelfth gives gain through institutions, if well-aspected, but usually indicates loss of fortune often with threat of imprisonment.

While the author does not have much confidence in it, the suggestion has been made that wealth will come late in life if the money planets are strong in the first, second, or third houses; between the ages of 40 and 50 if in houses four, five or six; between 30 and 40 if in houses seven, eight, or nine; and between 20 and 30 if in the tenth, eleventh, or twelfth houses. The author ignores this rule as he does the many others applicable to wealth and poverty, considering it far better to apply to the question of wealth and finance the same general principles of astrology set forth in these chapters.

Poverty

Certain other rules relating to poverty seem to have some application, although not strictly in line with the general astrological principles already mentioned, and they are submitted for the student's investigation and correlation through experience. According to these rules, poverty is indicated if:

1. The ruler of the second house is afflicted by Mars and Saturn or is weak by sign and is retrograde.

2. The cardinal signs are on the angles containing both Mars and Saturn.

3. Jupiter and Venus are in house six, retrograde, and either one rules the second house.

4. Too many planets are in masculine signs (this seems absurd to the author).

5. The Moon's South Node is in the second house, afflicted by Saturn.

6. Too many planets are retrograde (there is some truth in this, but it more often simply indicates disappointment).

7. Too many planets are below the horizon and heavily afflicted (in our opinion, these must be money planets).

Review Questions for Chapter 9

1. How do your vocational indicators coincide with your professional experiences?

2. What would be the value of knowing, early in life, of your latent talents and how far your abilities would extend?

3. How is wealth a relative matter in life?

4. Would the information about an individual's financial potential be of assistance to an employer, to an investor, or a lender?

5. Which houses are most involved with material resources?

| Chapter 10 |

Travel Relationships

Houses three and nine, known as travel houses, signify short or long journeys, although this may seem an arbitrary division of the mundane sphere. However, this is not the case for there is a definite relationship between spiritual intelligence and long journeys. Travel ultimately means the extension or expansion of information, whether this be physical travel or mental traveling in the sense of making an invention or discovery. Travels of the mind in relation to the third house become practical intelligence. Information obtained through journeys also gives an opportunity to broaden the intelligence generally.

Long journeys, whether physical or mental, tend to hasten psychological, religious, and spiritual development. It is often said that travel is educational and the greater the distance traveled the greater will be the stimulus to psychological development due to absorption of a different mode of life in foreign lands. It is a truism that the widely traveled individual is more learned than the unread rustic. Hence the premise in astrology is rooted in psychological and spiritual experience, as it should be.

Houses of Travel

The rules for synthesizing travel in the horoscope are simply an amplification of principles already discussed and which must be applied to houses three and nine, the signs on their cusps, the planets in them, the planets ruling the signs on the cusps, the house in which the rulers are found, and the aspects to these planets. Thus, cardinal signs on houses three and nine preeminently indicate travel; mutable signs indicate less travel; and fixed signs say comparatively little travel.

If the planets in houses three and nine are active and changeable, such as the Moon, Venus, Mars, Uranus, Neptune, and Pluto, they predispose to much travel. The Sun, Jupiter, and Saturn are less inclined to cause journeys. In the case of Mercury, it is necessary to study the nature of the planet most strongly influencing it.

But other considerations are also involved for travel is indicated when the rulers of houses three and nine are in cardinal signs, in the angles of the chart, or when rising, especially. The nature of travel, that is, whether for business, pleasure, or health, is determined by the house positions of the planets ruling houses three and nine, together with their aspects, and the houses ruled by the planets aspecting these rulers.

Furthermore, planet groups in a sign or house have a general impact. A majority of planets in cardinal signs indicates a tendency to much travel; in mutable signs says less travel; and in fixed signs gives very little travel. Care must be exercised in travel if malefic planets are found in houses three or nine, or else rule these houses.

If the rulers of houses three and four are more strongly placed than the ninth and tenth house rulers, the native will do better to remain near his or her birthplace or native land. The same is true if houses three and four are stronger than the ninth and tenth. But if the reverse shows to be true, that is the rulers of the ninth and tenth houses, or these houses themselves, are stronger than houses three and four, then the native will generally do well to live away from his or her birthplace or native country.

Planets in the Third House

Some astrological researchers have set out general principles concerning travel in connection with the houses which can be summarized as:

Sun in the third means it is better to stay at home.

Moon in the third gives many short, and sometimes unwanted, journeys.

Mercury in the third tells whether there will be any mental benefits from travel.

Venus in the third gives frequent pleasure trips.

Mars in the third predicts accidents while traveling by land.

Jupiter in the third suggests it is more profitable to remain near the birthplace.

Saturn in the third gives a lack of desire for travel on long journeys; can also indicate a tendency for motion sickness.

Uranus in the third suggests sudden journeys, danger of railroad accidents, and a fear of traveling by airplane.

Neptune in the third gives a restlessness at homes.

Pluto in the third indicates travel for mysterious reasons or encountering strange experiences while on the road.

Planets in the Ninth House

Sun in the ninth means an influential position abroad is possible.

Moon in the ninth is fond of travel.

Mercury in the ninth indicates whether there is mental benefit from travel.

Venus in the ninth suggests much tourist travel.

Mars in the ninth suggests accidents at sea or on long-distance flights.

Jupiter in the ninth says there is a successful residence abroad.

Saturn in the ninth gives a desire to travel to some distant place, which may not be fulfilled. The native is more likely to travel when old than when young.

Uranus in the ninth means sudden journeys, journeys to strange lands, and possibility of explorations.

Neptune in the ninth gives long sea trips or a life by the sea.

Pluto in the ninth gives travel of foreign nature but with some restrictions, such as travel during wartime. Explosions are possible near the native (note aspects).

These brief indications are especially valuable in interpreting the progressed horoscope, as the question is often asked whether a given period of life is favorable for travel.

Ruler of the Third House

When the ruler of the third house is in the various other houses it connotes the purpose of short distance trips.

Ruler of the third in the first means that journeys and moves are on behalf of brothers and sisters.

Ruler of the third in the second gives frequent short journeys to straighten out financial affairs.

Ruler of the third in the third brings trips for educational seminars or weekend workshops. These natives sometimes travel vicariously through novels or travel journals.

Ruler of the third in the fourth travels for property or family matters. There are frequent visits or telephone calls to parents.

Ruler of the third in the fifth brings pleasure trips and vacations to exciting places such as resorts.

Ruler of the third in the sixth is camping with the family. Beware of poison ivy or unclean water.

Ruler of the third in the seventh means travel with the mate.

Ruler of the third in the eighth can bring trips to relatives's funerals as well as business trips with the mate.

Ruler of the third in the ninth brings visits to or from relatives who have married foreigners.

Ruler of the third in the tenth gives a lot of short business jaunts.

Ruler of the third in the eleventh means going to conventions and meetings out of town.

Ruler of the third in the twelfth gives travel for health or to go on spiritual retreat.

Ruler of the Ninth House

Just as the ruler of third house describes short journeys, the ruler of the ninth house gives information about why the native is taking long trips.

Ruler of the ninth in the first means the native travels widely out of curiosity.

Ruler of the ninth in the second often works for an overseas shipping concern or an international banking interest and so must travel for financial reasons.

Ruler of the ninth in the third travels to write or to prove theories. This denotes a true explorer.

Ruler of the ninth in the fourth goes to other countries to study the cuisine. This is a scientific position which enables the native to be analytical. He goes back to childhood home for the last of life.

Ruler of the ninth in the fifth loves flying. There are many pleasure jaunts to other lands. Sometimes this is a government representative.

Ruler of the ninth in the sixth can travel to study the hygiene and food conditions of other countries. This also indicates working in the exporting business.

Ruler of the ninth in the seventh means going overseas to visit relatives of the spouse.

Ruler of the ninth in the eighth gives gain from long journeys concerning the possessions of deceased persons. This also indicates fleeing to escape persecution.

Ruler of ninth in the ninth indicates that the native teaches in a foreign university, is on a sabbatical journey to research a project, or travels overseas.

Ruler of the ninth in the tenth gives travel to receive honors or to accept an office.

Ruler of the ninth in the eleventh means the native makes fortunate friendships on voyages or overseas flights. He knows a lot of foreigners and may live for long periods in the home of a native of another country.

Ruler of ninth in the seventh seeks seclusion for personal development through travel.

Signs of Travel

The signs on the cusps of houses three and nine tell a lot about the type and frequency of travel the native can expect.

Aries on the third brings a lot of short-distance travel which the native prefers to handle by car. Some of the jaunts are business related but others are to satisfy the innate desire to explore new places. This individual is advised to satisfy the innate desire to explore new places. This individual is advised to avoid accidents by being *more* patient while driving.

Taurus on the third definitely prohibits much travel, especially if any discomfort might be involved. When this native absolutely must get away from home he likes for all the plans to be made in advance and all creature comforts taken good care of. In the past, this was one of the frequent riders on deluxe railroad trains touring this country.

Gemini on the third enjoys travel any which way. The individual will go by car, rail, or bus to see as much of the countryside as possible. There is a lot of short-distance travel but only a little long-distance.

Cancer on the third increases the short and medium length trips appreciably. There is travel both for business and pleasure with comforts requested. Details are planned months ahead of time if possible and plenty of luggage is taken along.

Leo on the third enjoys driving in order to look at the scenery. The native prefers being among the hills and mountains to the plains. Travel is somewhat restricted.

Virgo on the third complains but enjoys traveling anyway. He fusses at all delays whether to his own car or the rail service. The primary dislike for this native is having to change the water and food to which he is accustomed.

Libra on the third likes to travel with a mate or loved one. He primarily enjoys going by rail or air and likes to spend some time sightseeing. Many trips may combine business and pleasure.

Scorpio on the third would really enjoy one of the long sea voyages which were possible in earlier years. This love of luxury while traveling must be curtailed today and instead the native settles for luxurious lodging at night.

Sagittarius on the third likes the change and excitement of driving or sea travel. This sign greatly increases the distances possible to cover in a lifetime.

Capricorn on the third prefers to travel by rail in comfort. However, driving his or her own car is secondary when necessary business or social concerns mean traveling.

Aquarius on the third is the true explorer. This individual will dash out on a momentary weekend flight with a friend or will canoe up the rapids to explore a gorge.

Pisces on the third gets off schedule frequently to see something of interest. This individual really enjoys sailing on lakes or inland waterways in a private craft, but will settle for his own car when necessary. As long as there is a lot of mobility the native enjoys traveling no matter what the distance.

Long distance and overseas travel is really the opening of the mind to a change of customs, variance of locale, exciting new cuisine, and an entirely different approach to life. Whether the distance is great or small matters not as much as these other factors in determining a ninth house experience. Any occurrence that forces the native to learn about new ways and revise his daily habits is a learning or mind-expanding event shown by the ninth house in the horoscope. Signs on the cusp of that house have an effect on what the individual may expect to happen during his lifetime.

Aries on the ninth brings the desire to travel long distances but the event depends on how much effort the native is willing to expend to raise necessary finances. Air travel appeals to this native.

Taurus on the ninth loves to live in luxury while traveling. Both personal comfort and ready funds will determine the frequency of trips for this person. Sea travel on a luxury liner would be ideal.

Gemini on the ninth may travel hundreds of miles over multiple short jaunts during a year's time rather than take one long trip. There is a great desire to travel but this person is often forced, by circumstances, to see his own country first.

Cancer on the ninth does quite a bit of travel often with family members in tow. Overseas travel may be made by either air or ship depending on which is more convenient at the time.

Leo on the ninth enjoys combining air and car when traveling for pleasure or business. Often there is need of more money than the native has when travel opportunities come along.

Virgo on the ninth means that necessary travel depends entirely on the available funds. To this person travel can become a chore rather than a pleasure.

Libra on the ninth brings love of travel but often thwarting of plans. However, being adaptable, this native is not overly disappointed at staying home.

Scorpio on the ninth travels when the demand exists providing there is sufficient money to go in style and comfort. Overseas journeys are indicated.

Sagittarius on the ninth indicates much long-distance travel in a lifetime, either transoceanic or space travel. This is the most mobile combination in the horoscope. There may even be a permanent move abroad for the native.

Capricorn on the ninth shows long-distance travel by both land and water. Many business trips lead the native into other lands, whether they cross the ocean or not. During political campaigns they travel long distances in style.

Aquarius on the ninth means that travel depends on available funds or opportunities for this exploring person. There is interest in any form of air journeys.

Pisces on the ninth is the second most traveled placement. For this native a long cruise down a river or inland sea is as exiting as a transoceanic voyage or a trip to the Moon. Lucky circumstances occur which make it possible to travel even when monies are restricted. However, there is a warning to watch for trickery from foreign companions.

Multiple factors have been presented in this volume to assist in synthesizing the horoscope in order to best understand the native by character as well as to answer pertinent questions.

This completes the study of the natal horoscope and prepares the student for a branch called predictive astrology which will be presented in Volume IV of this textbook series.

Review Questions for Chapter 10

1. Have you any desire to travel long distances? Are these being fulfilled or are you discouraged about them? Does your horoscope explain the delay?

2. How does travel broaden the mind? Elaborate.

3. Look back over the early horoscopes which you erected in Volume I and add your present knowledge to the delineation. Has anything changed?

4. As you study astrology have your goals in life changed? Become more realistic? Become more understandable?

5. Do you have a different opinion of what astrology can and cannot do than you had when you began your course of study?

www.ingramcontent.com/pod-product-compliance
Lightning Source LLC
Chambersburg PA
CBHW020932180426
43192CB00036B/895